Dover Memorial Library
Gardner-Webb University
P.O. Box 836
Boiling Springs, N.C. 28017

D1111518

BASIC STEPS TOWARD COMMUNITY MINISTRY

GUIDELINES AND MODELS IN ACTION

By Carl S. Dudley

THE ALBAN INSTITUTE

BV
625
.D83
1991

Copyright © 1991 by Carl S. Dudley. All rights reserved. Reprinted 1992, 1993, 1997, and 2000.

This material may not be photocopied or reproduced in any way without written permission.

Library of Congress Catalog Card Number 91-72970

ISBN 1-56699-048-3

CONTENTS

Dover Memorial Library
Gardner-Webb University
P.O. Box 836
Boiling Springs, N.C. 28017

PREFACE

This book grows from a decade of experience helping congregations to develop strong, effective community ministries. Through the Center for Church and Community Ministries (associated with McCormick Theological Seminary) a team of clergy and lay leaders has worked with dozens of different parishes for periods of several years. What follows in these pages draws on our mutual learnings as congregational leaders have built ways to live out their commitments in ministries of compassion and justice.

We work with a wide variety of Christian congregations—mainline, evangelical, and Catholic parishes; in metropolitan centers, small cities, and rural communities; Anglo, African-American, Hispanic, and Asian cultures. Most are typical churches—not already heavily involved in social issues but willing to begin or expand a ministry program. We are grateful to the Lilly Endowment for their strong support of the program that made it possible for Center staff to work closely with these churches and for providing initial funding to develop programs addressing the survival needs of marginalized people in education, housing, health, unemployment, and reconciliation ministries.

From these experiences we developed a sequence of simple guidelines for the initial steps in building social ministries. To illustrate how the guidelines work, we have collected examples of how these church groups have used them. The examples I give on the following pages are drawn from reports written by local teams of clergy and lay leaders as they translated our guidelines into their settings. These passages give voice to the perceptions and commitments of local church leaders who have mobilized the strength of their congregations in developing community social ministries.

Together the guidelines and the examples provide an array of resources for congregational leaders to use in shaping your own ministries without the need for consultants or staff assistance. You need not remember all of the examples, but you will see how others have faced a variety of problems so that you can study more carefully some options for dealing with immediately relevant issues.

This do-it-yourself approach reaffirms the capacity of typical churches to develop uniquely effective ministries when grown naturally in their own appropriate style.

Alternate Procedure

You need not go through all the steps—like jumping through the hoops —before you respond to a particularly obvious need for community ministry. From our experience I have listed the essential elements for mobilizing social ministry, the foundations to be built, in whatever order seems appropriate. You may wish to begin with a study of identity rather than context, or begin with the study of people rather than boundaries. If you have already begun your ministry, or been working at it for a long time, these steps may provide a review of what you have done and fresh energy as you continue. By picking and choosing you may find ways to strengthen your ministry, set it in a larger context, or discover additional resources. We are not advocating a formula for ministry, but a selection of working tools to be used in ways that only you know best.

Appreciation

In the light of so many options, I should thank a few of the people who made this book possible. The primary gifts were from the leaders of these congregations who shared so generously with us from the depth and diversity of their experiences. I am continually impressed and renewed by the hard efforts and simple joys of people working together in ministry. Substantial support from the Lilly Endowment, made available through the creative vision of Robert W. Lynn, Senior Vice President for Religion at the time, stimulated and gathered these gifts. In the preparation of this manuscript, the staff of the Center for Church and Community Ministries was invaluable: Sue Corcoran in her tenacity in transcribing church and project reports; the detailed comments of William Boerman-Cornell, Sally A. Johnson, and Susan Sporte; and the common sense guidance of Donna Rose, Tracy Heaton de Martinez, and Thomas Van Eck. Alban Institute Editorial Advisory Council members Davida Foy Crabtree, Carolyn D. Minus, and Douglas Alan Walrath contributed useful insights and suggestions, and Celia Allison Hahn was especially helpful in many phases of developing and focusing this book.

INTRODUCTION

All sorts of congregations engage in compassionate outreach to help people in need and to change conditions that need changing. They may organize and support similar programs, but the ways they explain their ministries are different, unique to their congregation's own character and compelling to many of its members.

This book suggests a set of guidelines for developing social ministries and shows how congregations interpret and use them differently. A wide variety of congregations contributed their perspectives—Protestants and Catholics; liberals and conservatives; large and small membership churches; from various economic, ethnic, and cultural communities; located in cities, suburbs, towns, and open country. Each group has translated the guidelines, and together they help us understand how different groups can organize for ministry in their own cultural settings.

Parishes become involved in social ministries for many reasons. Some ministries respond to the needs of families and individuals in their community, some reflect the fear of changes in the church neighborhood, some result from the efforts of a few committed members, and others seek to recruit new church members. Most congregations act from a mixture of motives, but their ministries of concern are virtually always a natural expression of their Christian faith.

Jesus began his ministry with these compassionate words from the prophet Isaiah:

The Spirit of the Lord is upon me, because he has anointed me to preach good news to the poor. He has sent me to proclaim release to the captives and recovery of sight to the blind, to let the oppressed go free, to proclaim the year of the Lord's favor (Luke 4:18-19).

Churches create community ministries in response to the great commandments: You shall love the Lord your God with all your heart, and with all your soul, and with all your mind, and with all your strength . . . and you shall love your neighbor as yourself (Mark 12:30-31). They are trying to live out the expectations of our Lord that we will feed the hungry, clothe the naked, welcome the stranger, and minister to the infirm and imprisoned—remembering that "just as you did it to one of the least of these who are members of my family, you did it to me" (Matthew 25:40).

In response, congregations have generated a wide variety of social ministries, from soup kitchens and food pantries to shelters for the elderly and educational enrichment for children and youth. Other church groups have launched justice ministries that advocate for minority rights and social responsibility. This book tells how congregations have put their faith into action.

The Base: A Committed Group of Concerned Christians

Ministries of compassion and justice do not happen until someone cares enough to act. No amount of pressure and no organizational procedure can make someone love another enough to step forward and help. Pain, hardship, loss, and sadness are often triggers for sensitive Christians. Sometimes we worry about our own conditions, and that concern expands to include others as well. When poverty wears a child's face, when a friend is unemployed, when the children or the elderly or the broken families are real to us—then, by the strange power of the Holy ✓ Spirit, their pain may trigger the necessary energy and endurance in us to organize a ministry in response. As one church member discovered, "It hurts more when you know their names."

Social ministry begins with one or two individuals who care, but they must gather others who share their hopes for touching individuals, changing systems, and empowering people. This act of faith provides the foundation and sustaining energy for building a new ministry. The group may be official or informal, it may be homogeneous or diverse, it may focus on a specific ministry or share a wider concern for the welfare of the community—but the members of this group must be willing to make the development of this ministry a priority in their lives.

We cannot explain the supernatural chemistry which energizes people for ministry, but we can recount the experiences of those who cared and show how they went about it in ways appropriate to their own setting. As you read the examples from their churches, look for the unique phrases and styles that capture the essence of that group of people in their own setting and effectively mobilized their congregation to support a new ministry.

The Task, an Overview

In order to build a solid foundation for your ministry, your group needs to address three interdependent topics. The first is your social context, the place and people around your church. While your community context does not determine your ministry, it provides the framework of social forces, lifestyles, and community resources within which your ministry takes place. Second is your congregational identity, that unique character of the faith, history, and personality of the church. Congregational identity reflects the core values and commitments that shape your church and guide its response to the challenges of change. The third is organization, with leaders and resources, that gives your ministry the capacity to act—to respond to your context in ways consistent with your identity.

Therefore, this book is structured around the interaction of context, identity, and organization. Together these three elements are essential to gaining the commitment of any congregation to a community ministry. For your parish to support the ministry, three things need to happen: (a) Members of the congregation must see the community as their "turf," their responsibility, and accept the need for the ministry you target (social context). (b) Members must respond to this need as a natural and significant part of their Christian commitment (congregational identity). (c) Members must have the managerial capacity to respond to that need in a way that can make a difference in people's lives (organization). For an expanded description of these elements, see *The Handbook for Congregational Studies,* edited and co-authored by Jackson W. Carroll, et al. (Nashville: Abingdon Press, 1986).

These three elements are interdependent and interactive, and, in a sense, they must happen at the same time. Most groups, however, choose to concentrate on one aspect at a time.

The Dialogue between Guidelines and Examples

To help congregations mobilize social ministries, I offer a set of guidelines for exploring and building on your social context, congregational identity, and organization for ministry. In each area I suggest several steps or aspects that have been helpful with other congregations and comment briefly on their applications, limitations, and possible dangers. In conclusion I include a brief bibliography for further study.

But procedures alone are insufficient. In each area I offer brief examples of how different congregations have used these guidelines and what they have learned. This book, then, is a kind of dialogue between prescription and description, between the general statement of what might be done and glimpses of what particular churches actually have done. These examples offer windows through which we can see a variety of groups in action, planning social ministries. I've provided a thumbnail sketch of participating congregations and ministry projects in the appendix.

You might think of these as snapshots from our church family album. Like photographs, these excerpts highlight particular features, set in the appropriate social context. Therefore I have set in bold print a few words or phrases to convey what is unique or especially important in that example. The value of these examples is not in their similarities, but in the sometimes subtle differences that customize generic guidelines to fit the unique character of that particular setting for ministry. You may not want to read them all straight through, but rather pick and choose, focusing specifically on those areas that speak directly to your situation. I hope these illustrations will tickle your imagination, and, liberated from the oppression of a foreign formula for planning, you can find your own best way.

PART I

Social Context

People launch community ministries because they care—not just rationally, but with powerful compassion. When church members become concerned about church neighbors, when we recognize that problems must be faced, then community analysis can be helpful. In the strong, sustaining love of God, discovering that we care about our community is the first and basic foundation of social ministry.

Contrary as it may sound, our faith requires us to begin developing social ministry with a tough-minded community analysis. To share with others in building ministry, we must see the world as clearly as possible. Otherwise our familiarity and our prejudices will bind us to the past and blind us to problems, trends, and new possibilities. Social analysis of our context begins with the honesty that is essential to Christian ministry.

A community study should:

— displace our concern from ourselves to others around us;
— support and/or challenge what we expected to find;
— help us see changes and trends in our community;
— bring out into the open the hopes and fears that have only been whispered privately;
— provide a basis for focusing our social ministries;
— locate resources and allies that share our commitments;
— set our particular concerns in a regional and world context; and
— provide contacts and materials to help us interpret our ministry to a wider audience.

In community analysis we use a progression of steps that move from gathering more objective information, to reflection and probing the information, to the point where your committee can make preliminary decisions on the focus of ministry. In the initial data gathering, I offer two steps that focus first on places and then on people. Some committees may want to begin with a focus on people (step two), but I suggest that you first define the boundaries of your community and then describe the people who inhabit it.

STEP ONE: Define Your Community. You can define your community from many perspectives, but we will focus on three: (a) chart the physical boundaries, (b) identify the anchor institutions, and (c) look for the gathering places.

STEP TWO: Identify the People. I suggest three perspectives: (a) observe populations and lifestyles, (b) note historical changes and current trends, and (c) review statistical summaries.

Once you gather the basic information that defines the community and describes the people, your committee should move to a second level of reflecting on the material and probing its implications. For many groups, the interesting—perhaps explosive—material comes through in their follow-up explorations. Steps three, four, and five are related: as you recognize invisible people you can begin to trace the intangible forces, and your sensitivity to both will be expanded by the people you interview.

STEP THREE: Find the "Invisible" People. Every community has people who are ignored, marginalized, or simply out of sight. By identifying these groups, your committee and the congregation become more sensitive to a range of conditions in your community.

STEP FOUR: Analyze the Intangible Forces. Just as churches have always been concerned with spiritual forces, you should identify the social, economic, political, and religious forces operating in your community. These forces may be intangible, but they are real incentives and barriers in the lives of the people you are trying to reach and in the development of your ministry.

STEP FIVE: Listen to Your Community. Based on this wealth of data and feelings, you can initiate conversations with a wide variety of people from every segment of community life.

The final level of analysis invites you to draw together the themes of your study and insights of your conversations to make a tentative choice for a social ministry. Note that the same issues that you uncover in community study are relevant as your church seeks to reach out in a variety of ministries, from pastoral care to evangelism, from Vacation Bible School to stewardship of community resources. For each program you may shift the focus of your study, but basic questions remain: What are your natural, functional communities, and who are your marginalized peoples? What are the most evident human needs, and how effective is your community response? What does the Gospel call you to do, and who might be allies in this ministry?

STEP SIX: Choose Your Focus of Ministry. Although a firm decision on the appropriate ministry depends on finding a comfortable fit between your social context and your congregational identity, we encourage you to bring your community analysis into focus by deciding on a possible ministry (or ministries). This preliminary inclination toward a particular ministry will greatly facilitate your later discussions.

Define Your Community

The first task in gathering information is to define your community. Often this challenges our Christian conscience, reminding us that all people of the community are—or should be—the focus of our concern in Jesus Christ.

How then will you define your community? To combine the objectivity of study with the compassion of faith, we use three complementary approaches: (a) chart the physical boundaries, (b) identify the anchor institutions, and (c) look for gathering places. These approaches move us from the objectivity of an observer through the framework of institutions to the intimacy of belonging that holds the community together. You may gather extensive data, but you can summarize in two or three pages, along with the maps and documents that bring it to life. For extensive background in this approach you may wish to consult *Studying Your Community* by Roland Warren (Russell Sage Foundation, 1959).

Chart the Physical Boundaries

Guidelines

Boundaries are the easiest and most obvious starting point for identifying your community. Physical boundaries include major streets, highways, and railroad tracks or natural barriers such as hills, valleys, and rivers. When your committee agrees on your community boundaries, you will have a basis for visualizing the community together throughout your study.

For most churches there was a time when the members lived in the community and knew the neighborhood. But American economic and social mobility has confused such simplicity, and now many members no longer live in the old community. Therefore most churches, both Protestant and Catholic, need to identify both the immediate area in which they provide primary service to people in need and a larger region where their members live. The terms sometimes become confusing, since some Protestants call the smaller service area a "parish," while Catholics are more likely to use "parish" for a larger area of membership residence. In our work we use parish to refer both to the members who live in the area and to their concern for ministry to everyone in their community.

Even as you define your community to help you choose your ministry, so also your selection of ministry may help you define your community. As these examples from churches suggest, ministry and community are closely related.

Examples from Churches

A suburban church bordering a major city defines its parish boundaries in this way. Notice how their sense of mission helps to define their service community:

The boundaries of our church project service area is Calumet Park, with portions of the city overlapping to the north and east starting north to 119th, south to 131st, east to Halsted, and west to Winchester. We wanted to include the portions of Chicago to the north and east because:

1. They are our neighbors.
2. We have members in those surrounding areas.
3. It is a part of our outreach ministry program.
    (Calumet Park Covenant Church)

Sometimes physical barriers define the parish, and the church must make the most of it:

The physical boundaries of railroad tracks and switching yards, heavy industry, the White River, and Central State Mental Hospital *isolate the neighborhood from surrounding areas of the city as well as divide it internally. **This isolation and internal division (exacerbated today by racial boundaries) had made political and community organizing difficult.** It has only been in the last few years that basic city services like repair of streets and sidewalks, Crime Watch, and Community Development Block Grant programs have been available to us. (Washington Street Presbyterian Church)*

Concerned Christians in a rural community define their community and service area in a somewhat different way—by a combination of geography, geology, and history that reflects their orientation to their land. Notice how they still conclude with defining their service area by their concern for ministry:

*Our community is . . . situated in the northeast corner of Stark County in Osceola Township. The town rests on a large fertile plateau geologically known as the Camp Grove Ridge since the ridge was formed by a glacial deposit. The **service area** of our project would take in a ten-mile radius around and including our town. Within this area are what might easily be termed **pockets of poverty. These are small burgs that once were incorporated villages that due to population losses are no longer viable communities providing even the minimum of services.** (Leet Memorial United Methodist Church and Boyd's Grove United Methodist Church)*

Some kinds of ministry must be located not with geography but rather with a particular population that transcends location. In this example, the absence of physical boundaries becomes part of their identity:

*We were dealing with a **non-geographical community, namely the community of deaf and hearing impaired persons.** "Because their communications access to the hearing world is limited, deaf and hearing impaired persons tend to socialize together and . . . most deaf adults marry other deaf adults. **This pattern of socialization and intermarrying identifies the reality of a deaf culture in many cities across the country. Deaf people have . . . a sense of community.**" (Ridge Lutheran Church)*

Clarity about location strengthens most community ministries. When you have agreed on your boundaries, you may want to make a simple map of the area. But physical characteristics alone do not define a community. In many places major institutions are more influential in shaping people's lives.

Identify the Anchor Institutions

Guidelines

In many communities, significant institutions shape a way of life. These anchor institutions are often ignored by the citizens, who seem to accept them as "the way things are around here." But institutions like schools, hospitals, prisons, military bases, and recreational facilities can define the community in the same way that rivers and mountains define the land.

Such institutions are more than sources of employment; they shape the mood, the needs, the rhythm, and the attitudes of a community. They make a difference even for people who are not directly dependent upon them. They are especially significant for people who want to challenge or change the political or economic establishment.

Anchor institutions provide basic sources of power and decision making in the community. By "anchor institution" we imply our ambivalence. Like a ship's anchor, they provide stability in a storm. But they may also prevent us from moving forward in calm or changing times. In your social analysis, identify these major institutions and explore their implications for your ministry.

Examples from Churches

This church group, located in an agrarian town, easily identifies several anchor institutions that hold the community in place and provide its basic livelihood:

> *The major institutions in this community are education, farming, industry, and retirement. In addition to six public schools, there is a small church-related college with 1,000 students and one private grammar school . . . Farming is also a large institution in the area.*

*Like most farmers, agriculturalists are suffering economic hardship
here, and the small family farm is giving way to agribusiness.*

*Industry has experienced a decline over the last 15 years, but
still provides a substantial number of jobs and revenue. We have an
oil refinery, a book bindery, a foundry, a playground equipment
manufacturer, a plastics producer, a grain elevator, a veal feed
distributor, and several smaller plants. Retirement is one of our
largest institutions. In a town of 6,000 people, there are two large
retirement homes with church affiliation. A Presbyterian home
houses 300 residents and the Church of the Brethren home hosts
175 retirees. Together the homes employ more than 200 workers in
the health, domestic, and food service industries.*

*The College is the largest employer and the largest contributor
to the economic base of the community . . . The presence of a college
in a small town makes for greater diversity in life here, but also
creates an uncomfortable disparity between those with a post-
secondary education and those without. (Manchester Church of the
Brethren)*

Some churches recognize a single or dominant pivot for economic,
social, and often political stability in their community. In the following
examples from churches, both reflect a natural ambivalence about the
dominant community institutions. The first recognized its economic
dependency, and the second saw how much the institution affected their
social life as well:

*Kokomo can be simply described as a predominantly blue collar,
union-oriented city . . . Delco Electronics and the Chrysler trans-
mission plant . . . account for approximately 40% of the jobs, and
the other local industries are dependent upon these two simply
because a major portion of their business is as suppliers. As Delco
and Chrysler go, so goes our economy. (St. Luke's United Methodist Church)*

*Many members of the congregation have connections to the State
Hospital through direct employment themselves or of a family
member. Local businesses and professionals profit from sales and
referrals. In addition . . . some former patients have decided to
relocate in town . . . They often lack skills for independent living,*

*nor are they able adequately to speak and demand services for themselves. **Due to their poverty, they become part of the poor, disenfranchised townspeople . . . and many ex-patients live within the church neighborhood.** (Baptist Temple)*

Unfortunately these institutions are most evident when they make changes which threaten the community. Such changes often provide the basis for developing ministry. This report laid the groundwork for a ministry with broken families and battered women:

*Economically, the **loss of the steel industry** has changed the stable character of the area; as jobs go, so do the people . . . Further, there are taverns on every third corner in the residential streets surrounding the church. The rate of alcoholism is high. **Family unity is threatened** by the sudden "poverty" brought on by the mills closing. **This area, once proud and prosperous, has lost its sense of identity and direction.** (South Chicago Covenant Church)*

Look for Gathering Places

Guidelines

In every community there are places where people gather for economic, social, political, and religious activities. Churches are obvious gathering places, as are parks, schools, service clubs, taverns, and street corners. Not only restaurants but local businesses can also be gathering places, well-worn spots where neighbors exchange greetings and gossip along with goods and services. Your community analysis should include a survey of the businesses and agencies that serve the community and the churches and voluntary groups that reflect the values of the residents.

In surveying the community gathering places, you will find an affinity with some particular groups and locations. You may be attracted to the gathering places where you are personally comfortable or to locations where other distinct groups are known to gather. In the features you select, this exercise will allow you to lift up community problems which may be the first clear indication of the issues that your ministry will eventually address.

Most churches list other churches in their surveys of gathering

places. Generally, committee members gravitate toward those churches
that depend upon similar theological or social strata of community life,
not because they have worked together, but more often because they
have competed with these churches for prospective members. Yet in this
new ministry other congregations may become allies and partners.
Cooperation in social ministries can be deeply satisfying; it can provide a
common ground for transcending differences, easing tensions, and
sharing the movement of the Spirit in our midst.

Examples from Churches

The following three examples seem to catch the unique beat—and
perhaps even the melody—of community life in each location. The first
is from a small river town in middle America where the proud past lives
on, but the social fabric of the rural economy is struggling for survival.
Notice the historic and political tint to these gathering places:

> *In the County are 33* **churches** *. . . [and] five* **school systems** *(k-12).
> Other features of the county include the Marshall-Putnam* **Farm
> Bureau**, *Marshall County* **Historical Society**, *three* **nursing homes**,
> *four major grain elevators, the light company, committees for* **both
> political parties, 4-H groups and the County Extension Office**.
> *Marshall County has the* **oldest annual celebration in the state**, *Old
> Settlers Day, which was first held in 1870. The most significant
> socio-economic feature of the community has been agriculture . . .
> (Immaculate Conception Catholic Church)*

If you read between the lines you might have guessed that this social
ministry generated support for a large community building that is now
used by all age groups, especially the elderly.

Comparing that rural survey to the view of an urban group, we see
increased specialization and a growing tension in franchise operations
that threaten local merchants. The committee members begin with
businesses they know, then move on to social clubs and neighborhood
activities, and finally note what they consider the active churches. Later
these layers of neighborhood networks provide the strategy for the congregation's approach to community support for their social ministry:

> *Businesses in the service area include a major bank **branch**, a credit union, two **owner-operated** funeral homes, an **independent** insurance agency, a CPA, one doctor's office, one lawyer's office, two small **owner-operated** grocery stores, two printing companies, one **owner-operated** bakery, two fast-food **chain** restaurants, two **locally operated** restaurants, one tavern/restaurant, one **owner-operated** barber shop, several beauty shops (some operating out of homes), and one convenient dairy/ice cream **franchise**. An **AFL/CIO union hall, a fire station, a city park, and several service fraternities**, including a VFW Masonic Lodge and Rebekah and Oddfellows Lodge, are located in the . . . service area. **The active churches** in the area include [ours], St. Anthony's Catholic, Washington Street Methodist, St. Luke's Chapel, Missionary Baptist and Hawthorn Baptist Chapel. (West Park Christian Church)*

The third survey picture is equally urban, but reflects a mixture of middle class and marginal households in an African-American community. What begins as a simple list of businesses becomes a vivid picture of community activity that challenges people to support their outreach ministry:

> *Small businesses in the area are: five beauty shops, two barber shops, a grocery store, cleaners, TV repair shop, fish market, service station, neighborhood tavern, restaurant, **three or four pea shake gambling joints, a 500 liquor store** . . . **The community's changing trends include deteriorating and boarded buildings**, traffic blockage by double-parked automobiles, commercial trucks at a local business, **and people on streets in "vice areas."** (Riverside Park United Methodist Church)*

Summary

When you have completed Step One you should have a brief report that summarizes your findings and defines your community through (a) the physical boundaries, (b) the anchor institutions, and (c) the gathering places. You may have gathered many pages of materials, but a summary of a few pages helps your committee to focus and provides materials that can be shared with others. You may also have gathered and constructed maps and other supporting documents that give visual impact to your brief report.

The strength of your report lies in finding those few key symbolic phrases and examples which capture community needs and resources in ways that are significant to the members of the congregation.

Identify the People

Relationships are at the center of the Christian faith—relationships with our Lord and within the church family. We can appreciate why many planning committees related more easily to people than to physical definitions of the community. We began with boundaries, institutions, and gathering places so that we could talk about the same people. Your committee might get into this section by telling stories of your experiences in living, working, struggling, suffering, and celebrating with the people around you.

Although stories of individuals may be the best way to get inside the lives of people, in order to shape a ministry we must associate individuals with larger groups based on characteristics they share. But how can we categorize them? We want to avoid stereotyping people and losing touch with the uniqueness of each person, yet some characteristics provide important categories that they themselves would claim:

— distinctive racial, ethnic, or cultural history;
— religious beliefs and affiliations with religious groups;
— education, employment, and income (class) differences;
— age, gender, and sexual orientation;
— family size, age, and life-cycle situation; and
— community location, size, and economic orientation.

We suggest three sources of information as you describe the people of your community: (a) observe populations and lifestyles, (b) note historical changes and current trends, and (c) review statistical summaries.

Observe Populations and Lifestyles

Guidelines

Describe the community by the people who inhabit it. Typically this is
an explosive task for your committee since the more familiar you are
with the area, the less likely you are to agree. Agreeing on this complex
tapestry of similarities, differences, events, and experiences can be
energizing and also exhausting.

Sometimes this discussion is awkward for the committee as members discover their strong and sometimes controversial feelings about
well-known citizens and particular segments of the community. We
rarely remember events in the same way, and our interpretations say as
much about us as about the people or events we are recalling. In this
discussion your committee members come to understand each other
better and to recognize the differences each one brings to the decisions
for ministry.

Community analysis requires the committee to test their memories
and experiences by a variety of contacts throughout the area. The
"windshield survey" is one popular method of summarizing your observations of the habits and lifestyles of community people. Your committee should spend time walking and driving through the community,
talking with people, and making notes on your observations and experiences. The only real experts on the community are the people themselves. The windshield survey is more than a quick drive through the
community; it reflects the committee's best wisdom on the people and
groups that might be seen by a sensitive, informed observer. You might
also ask yourselves how you would describe your community to an
outsider: what are the essentially human characteristics of your community?

Examples from Churches

These examples show four ways of seeing the people of the community.
The first is a middle class African-American neighborhood in a major
city, where the committee defines its neighbors by their similarity to the
church and also vice versa. Hard work, family values, and community
safety provide the bridge between the church and community and
foundations for their ministries:

*Our Church Community is a homogeneous group of **stable family
households**. There is significant communication and cooperation
among neighborhood residents. **Property values are stable and the
crime rates are relatively low** in our tract areas. [Our church]
shares many **common values and characteristics** with the surrounding community and therefore flourishes. [Our membership] is
composed of **hard-working black homeowners and household
renters**. More than fifty-percent are lifelong residents. (Martin
Temple A.M.E.Z. Church)*

From another part of the same large city comes a typical windshield
survey that describes the people in two quite different corridors:

*Edgewater and Uptown are two of the most racially diverse in the
city. As an example, Hayt Elementary has students with **16 different
native languages** . . . High-rise apartment buildings line the lake
front and house more **affluent residents**. Paralleling Sheridan just
one and two blocks to the west are Winthrop and Kenmore Streets
referred to in the community as the Winthrop-Kenmore Corridor . . .
the **housing area for the low or no income families**. Renovation
has been going on there for the last few years but the Corridor still
houses many low income residents of **different racial and ethnic
backgrounds**. (Immanuel Lutheran Church)*

The next windshield survey challenges any stereotypes we might
harbor as we drive through the bucolic beauty of rural America. What
were once homogeneous farming communities now feel divided socially,
abandoned economically, and fractured politically. This description laid
the groundwork for a ministry to recover and re-knit a sense of community:

*Two distinct socioeconomic groups of people live in the area. The
largest property owning group, **the permanent family farmer**, lives
in **well-kept rural dwellings**. They pay the major part of the taxes
and create seven of the thirteen farm related businesses located
within the project area. The church congregations are made up
largely from this group . . . The second group tends to be a **bedroom
community group**. They work and spend money outside the area*

*and return to sleep. They live in dwellings of various states of
repair and sizes and tend to be short-term residents.*

*The **community has no center** of industry, business, or shopping
. . . Communication such as telephone is supplied by **four ex-
changes that require long distance assistance.** Two county govern-
ments and several social agencies serve the community, but are
based outside the 4 townships. Few social organizations cross
county lines. (Deer Creek Presbyterian Church)*

Finally, a civic-minded congregation in a larger community uses
housing as an index of lifestyle and economic class. Their description
embraces even greater diversity, reflecting an inclination to think of
larger community-wide issues for ministry:

*Geographically, Kokomo can be easily divided into socioeconomic
regions . . .The **upper middle class** can be found in the southwestern
and northeastern corners of the city. The majority of these people
are two-income families of professional and semi-professional
workers. They live in conventionally-built homes and have children.
The **middle class** can be found in the west central and south central
part of the city. Many of these families have two incomes and are
blue collar workers. They live in prefabricated homes and seem to
spend most of their discretionary income on vehicles and recreation.*

*Although the **black community** lives predominantly in the east
central part of the city, blacks can be found in many other areas of
Kokomo also. There is no true ghetto in Kokomo. The blacks live in
35-year-old bungalows and two-story homes—some converted into
multiple family dwellings . . . The **lower economic class of whites**
can be found in the southeastern part of the city. The entire area is
run-down with the prefabricated homes in poor repair. There is
low-income government housing and a considerable amount of junk
strewn about. This area seems more depressed than the black area.
(St. Luke's United Methodist Church)*

Note Historical Changes and Current Trends

Guidelines

Your understanding of community will be incomplete if you focus only
on the present situation. A sense of history gives depth and meaning to
current conditions. Just as you began your study of populations with a
sharing of personal experiences, so you may be stimulated by sharing
your own memories of change and your awareness of trends. Douglas
Walrath, in *Planning for Your Church* (Philadelphia: Westminster,
1984), offers a process to push our memories from nostalgic lamenta-
tions to a positive and shared foundation for creative new ministries,
asking simply, What are the changes in the past five years and what do
you see for the future?

Where possible, you might form a subcommittee on history with
these same two tasks: one, to explore the roots of the present in the
extended events of the past and, two, to find the current trends that
suggest the shape of the future. History gives unique insight into the
causes for oppressive conditions; current trends help identify the unfold-
ing issues. Both are essential in the focus for your social ministry.

Strangely, your committee is most apt to bog down in the historical
study, partly because it is endless, but more because it is controversial.
A few committees become hypnotized by the information, but more
become gun-shy about conflicting viewpoints.

Approached with courage and fairness, your studies of history and
trends can stimulate congregational interest and help focus your ministry
where the need may be greater and the impact may correspond with tides
that shape the future of your community.

Examples from Churches

This white Protestant church uses a simple historical memory to remind
the congregation about current social and political realities of their
community. With this reminder the church began a new cooperative
ministry with a neighborhood Catholic church:

> [Our community] was originally a separate town in the farmlands to
> the northwest of Chicago. It was settled by **European immigrants**
> who established a town along the railway line . . . In particular,

*three groups settled here: Poles, Germans, and Irish, most of them
Roman Catholic. [We] remain a neighborhood with **strong ethnic
identities**. (Avondale Presbyterian Church)*

An African-American congregation remembers with bitter frustra-
tion their efforts to move into a previously all white community, but uses
their past crises for current energy:

*As blacks continued to move in, it set off an array of real estate
activity . . . Some realtors tried to have a sellathon by telling the
whites this was the last chance for top dollars, playing on their
fears. Others blocked advertising of houses for sale. Bankers/
mortgagors began redlining the area, refusing home loans and
improvements, etc. In spite of all this, **we survived and we are now
an integrated community, thanks to the help of some of the citizens**. (Calumet Park Covenant Church)*

When significant changes break into congregational consciousness,
they often point to issues that can be translated into ministries. In this
small town, the committee recognized a shift in employment patterns as a
basis for ministry with children:

*Through the years, there has been a shift from heavy dependence on
agriculture toward being a bedroom community whose residents
work largely outside the community. This has resulted in a **large
number of children of grade school age who have both parents
working outside the community** and not returning until about 6:00
p.m. Visible results of this can be seen in the number of **children
roaming the streets after school [and] . . . an increasing of vandalism in the community**. (Fisher United Methodist Church)*

Many churches point to positive changes in the community to build
optimism and support for their ministry. This city church sees a relationship between a population shift and new sidewalks, both signs of hope:

*The purchasing of **older homes by younger couples and families**
and the fixing-up of those homes is evidence of the upswing of the
area . . . **New sidewalks and curbs** are evidence of the city's interest
in the area. A more active young adult population (ages 25-40) is
becoming evident in the neighborhood and community center*

*programs and services, suggesting the emergence of a **more vital
neighborhood population with the education and resources to
create growth and change.** (Washington Street Presbyterian
Church)*

Review Statistical Summaries

Guidelines

Statistical materials have a reassuring, firm objectivity, especially in
comparison with our personal experiences and impressions. By reducing
attributes to numbers we can make comparisons among populations and
across time. We can introduce more kinds of information into the discussion. Your community study will be suspect if you fail to support
your concerns with statistics or, on the other hand, if statistics are all you
offer. Both narrative and statistical materials are essential.

Statistics are understandably offensive, especially in the church.
Statistics reduce people to digits and replace names with numbers. We
know, for example, that some basic issues cannot be reduced to numbers,
and some people are overlooked or ignored or have good reasons to
refuse to be counted. Often subjective judgments enter into the choice of
questions, the methods of study, the selection of data, and the style of
presentation. There are good reasons to worry about statistical reports.

Even with these limitations, statistical reports are important. They
broaden our base of information and include segments of the population
that might otherwise be ignored. Broadly based statistical information
will inform the committee, support the proposal to sponsoring groups,
and help you to interpret your ministry in the church and the community.

The primary source for statistical information is the U.S. Census,
even though its accuracy has been seriously challenged. Other sources
include libraries, schools, planning boards, utilities, and chambers of
commerce; in addition, a variety of government, business, professional,
social, and religious agencies collect specialized data. You do not need
much, but it must be on target for the questions you are asking.

Examples from Churches

To see the impact statistics can have, compare these two reports. Both represent farming communities with the same concerns, but the first report only discusses the issue, while the second supports its claim with the facts:

> *Being a rural community might lead one to assume that agriculture . . . has the greatest impact on the majority of residents. However, statistics indicate that lack of job availability on many levels is more likely to head the list of concerns. (West Street Christian Church)*
>
> *The projected population as of July 1, 1986, shows a decline in the population for almost all our towns . . . ranging from -.09 to -16.5%. The decline is due to the closing of several of the General Motor plants in our area . . . and also the decreasing number of farmers:*
>
> | | *1954* | *1964* | *1974* | *1982* |
> |----------------------|---------|---------|---------|---------|
> | *# of farms* | *2,297* | *1,621* | *1,346* | *1,126* |
> | *# of acres farmed* | *241,106* | *235,405* | *229,677* | *222,300* |
>
> *(St. Mary's Catholic Church, Alexandria)*

By contrast, this city parish uses statistics in two ways—first to develop a profile of community problems and then to compare its community with others. Even if we resist the first more formal approach, we are moved by the second:

> *[Our community] is fourteen square blocks with the following geographics according to the 1980 census:*
>
> — *Total population 6,309 in 2,586 households for an average household size of 2.4.*
> — *White: 37%, Black: 31%, Hispanic: 27%, Other: 5%.*
> — *2,420 of the households are renter occupied and 1,151 are without vehicles.*
> — *Average household income is $13,622 with a per capita income of $5,550 and a median income of $11,879.*
> — *61.3% of the households earn less than $15,000 per year.*
> — *30% of the population is under the age of 19; 47% is under the age of 24.*

*The Children's Defense Fund reports that children such as those who live in [our neighborhood] are "**twice as likely to die** in the first year of life, to see a parent die, to be suspended from school, and to be unemployed as teens. They are **three times as likely to be murdered** between the ages of five and nine, to be in foster care, and to die of known child abuse. They are **four times as likely to be incarcerated** between the ages of 15 and 19." (Good News Community Church)*

Statistics can also help us define nongeographic communities by their problems and common concerns:

*The **unemployment rate among the (deaf) population** was four times greater than that of hearing adults, and the level of employment was primarily fixed at unskilled or semi-skilled positions . . . Clearly one factor affecting the kinds of jobs deaf adults were finding was their limited educational opportunities. (Ridge Lutheran Church)*

Summary

When you finished Step Two, you should summarize your learnings in one or two pages, plus any materials you have gathered. Your report will describe the people of your community through (a) populations and lifestyles, (b) historical changes and current trends, and (c) supporting statistical summaries.

Exploring Below the Surface

Steps One and Two, defining the place and describing the people, are foundational for community analysis. They provide a solid basis to address the needs and issues of people you minister with. This descriptive and statistical information will help your committee decide about a ministry and interpret that program to potential supporters.

Many community studies stop at this point. People and places are significant, but most church groups need more time to probe the implications of their findings and explore the dynamics of community change. Steps three, four, and five ask you to look below the surface in three ways: find the invisible people, analyze the intangible forces, and listen to the community. These three areas of study feed each other, and they are best carried on simultaneously. For additional help in approaching these areas, see *Social Analysis: Linking Faith and Justice* by Joe Holland and Peter Henriot, S.J. (Maryknoll, NY: Orbis, 1983).

Your follow-up explorations will lead you to probe not only the life of your community, but also your own faith commitments. The question of invisible people encourages you to search for those who are most marginalized and in need of assistance. Sometimes that search reveals our own preconceptions or habitual blindness to people in pain or to sources of power.

As you analyze the intangible political, economic, cultural, or religious forces, your committee may uncover a variety of possible ministries. Intangible forces are often the least subject to documentation, the most sensitive in committee discussion, and the most significant in the choice and the development of your ministry.

Listening to the community is part of every step of social analysis. But when combined with your search for invisible people and your exploration of intangible forces, your interviews should contact more diverse groups of people and ask more focused questions.

Some church groups feel the urgency to begin ministry without further information gathering, discussion, and delay. The search for invisible people and intangible forces is not just an exercise to be completed en route to ministry, but a discipline of social awareness that should be incorporated in the working habits of every sensitive Christian ministry.

Find the "Invisible" People

Guidelines

The search for people who are invisible to you invites a fresh look at familiar turf. It helps you discover marginalized people whom you may have ignored—or seen so frequently that they have blended into the landscape.

Further, as we look at the community through the eyes of these invisible people, we see the church in a new and less complimentary light. We find ourselves asking new kinds of questions about ourselves and our Christian commitments. We take a closer look at the motivations and effectiveness of our church's mission and recognize more clearly our limitations.

Many churches celebrate these new discoveries and welcome the opportunity to respond. They use their new discoveries to generate energy in support of the ministries they choose. They see the need to help in ways that empower the alienated people and do not perpetuate the conditions they seek to change.

In fact, we limit social ministry when we begin by asking only, "What are the needs of people in our community?" This can be a condescending approach taken by people in positions of social, political, and economic power. We might better begin with the perspective of the √ marginalized, powerless, invisible people and ask, "What needs to be changed to make this a just society?" Or to put the question in a more prophetic form, "How can this society be helped to conform to the will of God?"

Examples from Churches

In refocusing on these marginal people, we may discover forms of
alienation, injustice, and oppression perpetuated by our community
neighbors and even church members. We begin to see failures in institutions we have trusted and people we know well. The sin in our systems
and in ourselves confronts us.

Students of the Bible have long recognized the special attention God
devotes to "widows and orphans," the biblical symbol of invisible people
in every society. Many churches have been energized to launch a social
ministry when they discovered the marginal lives of neighbors, especially the poor and elderly:

> *The invisible folk are the **elderly** . . . In many of the apartments
> older persons are present, but unseen. Many of the homes are
> owned by aged persons, some of whom have **neither the strength or
> financial resources** to maintain property. Some are in churches
> and participate in community groups, others seem to withdraw
> behind drapes and doors to watch TV. (Irvington United Methodist
> Church)*

> *[Our community] has been either fortunate, or unfortunate depend-
> ing on one's biases, in the area of low visibility of its poor. Many
> times hidden and off the main paths in the City, they are consigned
> to **pockets within the city**, as in the near south end. Their presence
> contradicts the comfort index of a great majority of the area's
> population and calls for better and more deliberate response from
> the city's institutions, public and private alike. (Lafayette Church of
> the Brethren)*

Churches also frequently mention physically and mentally handicapped people who have been de-institutionalized:

> *[Other] invisible persons could be **mental patients** discharged from
> Central State, who settle in the area with no established support
> network to help them establish stability, find employment, and
> become "visible" in the community. (Baptist Temple)*

Not all the invisible people are poor or handicapped. Many are long-time residents and even respected citizens who have been pushed by economic forces beyond their control. Consider this narrative from a community large enough to have many of the conditions of an urban area yet small enough for people to know each other's personal problems:

> *Some of the invisible people are the **unemployed and those affected by area layoffs**, as well as those urged by their companies into an unanticipated early retirement. The **new homeless forced out of homes by inability to pay mortgages** can be hidden in the households of relatives. **Teen-agers** barred from their parents' homes and moving from one friend's house to another could also be termed invisible. **Single parents** struggling with bills and survival issues fall in that category. The **elderly** for whom aging means increasing isolation become invisible to us too. There is no specific area that is considered or identified as a pocket of poverty, but invisible people are scattered throughout the community in their own **private pockets of poverty and deprivation**, unable to recognize their own powers to improve their situations. The isolation factor contributes to the lack of empowerment. (Community United Church of Christ)*

Not everyone finds or wants to find these hidden problems. Some committees doubt the existence of invisible people who need to be incorporated into the larger community:

> *It is **hard to identify any invisible people**. It appears that there are none. When contacting the local electric utility, they did not indicate that there was any visible problem to them. (Deer Creek Presbyterian Church)*

More frequently, however, the discovery of invisible people mobilizes a church to help them personally and to challenge the institutions that have contributed to their conditions:

> *The **invisible people** . . . **feel powerless**. In the senior citizens apartments . . . they feel insecure as the apartments' emergency cords only turn on the light in the hallway . . . Our committee found out these apartments were not subsidized and were supposed to be. We **wrote a few letters** to the Federal Housing Authority and **circulated a petition** among our churches. Within a few weeks the*

*rent was cut by $100 in most cases. They also **filled up the units** since it was not so costly. (Washburn Christian Church)*

Analyze the Intangible Forces

Guidelines

Your committee should plan at least one discussion of the social, economic, political, and religious forces operating in your community. Using the material you have gathered to date, set aside time to explore your options for ministry and the intangible forces that form incentives or barriers to each. Your discussion will probably include:

— laws that affect the groups of people you want to reach;
— mobility, prejudice, and possible limits on outsiders;
— cultural values toward family, education, and leadership;
— employment, changing markets, and future job security;
— "powers and principalities" of the local leader network;
— religious convictions and spiritual powers in our world; and
— personal and group awareness of oppression and affirmation.

We can easily identify intangible forces with sources of power in the community, such as dominating employers, entrenched political figures, dysfunctional educational systems, and the like. But we must also recognize the bias in our own perspectives. When our religious commitments come into conflict with our economic, political, and social self-interest—as often happens when we develop or work with a social ministry—our faith is measured more by what we do than what we say.

Examples from Churches

Intangible forces add a new dimension to the story of ministry, showing the muscle beyond the statistical or narrative descriptions. Frequently congregations with Hispanic or other immigrant people tell of unseen forces that shape their ministries:

> *Regardless of statistical changes or trends cited in the data given, there exists a major factor whose impact neither we nor the statisticians will be able to discern for some time to come. With the passing of* ***the new immigration law,*** *the future composition, direction, and progress of our community is uncertain. (Douglas Park Covenant Church)*

A discussion of intangible forces allows church members to wrestle with the differences between the official information and personal experiences. Sometimes the ripple of a trend is felt first by service institutions like the churches and the schools. The official census may say differently, but these people feel the first wave of a change developing:

> ***Our food distribution lines*** *are quite long these days. Five years ago the churches organized a food pantry. Before that most people had good jobs so there was simply no need for it. It is obvious that plant layoffs began a* ***vicious cycle of unemployment, hunger, and people moving away*** *looking for something better; as more moved, businesses closed in town and houses began being boarded up.* ***Business closing locally causes more unemployment and more empty houses.*** *(Washburn Christian Church)*

Intangible forces include the values we share that hold us together, sometimes made stronger in hardship:

> *Unemployment is very present . . . and local resources are declining . . . Some of our churches receive smaller contributions and some of our membership are seeking public assistance for the first time, yet they nevertheless continue to provide these much needed social services.* ***Our community is strong and . . . very supportive of the needs of its people*** *. . . As our United Way so aptly puts it, "Canton Is Special." (First Presbyterian Church, Canton)*

Intangible forces allow your committee to discuss directly the political and social attitudes that are more elusive in statistical and descriptive reports. This Protestant congregation recognized the weaving of politics and religion in the community and therefore joined with a Catholic group to develop a common ministry:

> *Springfield has an **"old guard,"** a **"good old boy"** network, established by lifelong residents of the community. More times than not, to acquire power in this political city you must have been born here. In addition, **the power brokers are largely Catholic**, not surprising when nearly half of the community is Roman Catholic . . . There are still the underlying problems of **racism, hunger, homelessness, poverty, and unemployment and the ramifications caused by these "conditions."** All the social ills of any metropolitan area are present here, and our church is being called to respond. (Hope Presbyterian Church)*

Prayer, biblical faith, and courage are essential ingredients for a congregation to strengthen individual voices to look as honestly at themselves as they do at the community they live in. The insights about ambivalence and capitulation in the following observations did not come from a single person, but reflect a continuing congregational dialogue about the health of their community:

> *Homeostasis, a "let it be" attitude [encourages] . . . apathy and unconcern. This overriding **sense of stability** has impacted our congregation in the same way it has impacted the general religious community . . . Church people, in response to their faith, are eager to help, to support from their material bounty. [However] . . . there has been a real **shying away from advocacy and challenging the structures that undergird the issues that need to be addressed** . . . The problems are bandaged without opening the sore for healing. (Lafayette Church of the Brethren)*

Discouragement, even despondency (or worse, apathy), often mark congregations that see no way to respond to the negative forces of their communities. But hope is more characteristic of congregations with social ministries, not because they believe that they are winning, but because they offer members at least an opportunity to express their faith in action:

> *Economic factors create the primary issues affecting our community. The layoffs in manufacturing, the farm crisis, and the nationwide recession result in many moving away, increased unemployment and underemployment, the need for both parents in a family to work, a decrease in family income, the failure of businesses, economic problems of small towns, and probably increased failures of marriage and a growing alcohol and drug abuse problem.* **A good result of these discouraging economic factors is a re-evaluation of values. People seem to be becoming more committed to family, church, social programs and more responsive to people in need.** *(Immaculate Conception Catholic Church)*

Listen to Your Community

Guidelines

With your background of exploring the community, your committee should become more intentional about your interviews. Your various maps of populations, institutions, and gathering places offer an array of contacts. Your reflections on invisible people and intangible forces should suggest a sharp focus to your inquiry. Your statistical support can add authority and bluntness to your dialogue. But, as always, you will gain more when you approach each interview as an informed listener who cares a great deal and who needs to learn what this individual (or group) can teach.

An amazing assortment of people are available and willing to talk with church committees about community ministries. You can reach educators, political figures, community planners, government agency staff, agencies, police officers and judges, business leaders and local shop keepers, labor officials, reporters, and caregivers in medicine and social services, in programs for the elderly, family, youth, and children. More challenging, you also need to talk with typical citizens who share your concerns (although not necessarily your viewpoint) but are unfettered by institutional connections.

You will find these interviews helpful in several ways. First, you will learn more than the facts of the community. As your committee discovers others who share your concerns and your feelings, you will form relationships with people who see common issues in different ways. You will discover and weave together a network of people who care about many of the same issues and who learn to work together even across your differences.

Second, others will see your church as a concerned neighborhood institution. The people you contact begin to think of the church as a potential partner in the areas of shared concerns. They will treat the church differently and include the church in community meetings it has not been invited to before.

Third, the members of your group begin to see themselves differently. Once they begin the interviews, they realize that they are changing in the process. As others begin to think of the church as a partner and ally, the committee members re-examine the church's ministry and mission. We often find a loop of growing self-confidence: when the church shows interest in the community, others accept the church, and church leaders begin to think and act in more inclusive ways.

You will find that, of all the material you have gathered in your community study, the interviews are the hardest to capture in print. In these interactive experiences, body language and feeling tones have equal impact with spoken words. Therefore, we suggest that your written reports of interviews be simple and brief: list the participants, summarize the conversation, and note any follow-up items and persons responsible.

Examples from Churches

These first reports are typical of local church interviews with leaders of agencies and institutions. Note the variety of people approached and the way these professionals summarize their concerns in an easy list for the committee to work on. You can see the networks begin to form and loops of self-confidence develop as the churches become more highly esteemed and the community leaders want to be kept informed:

> *When one of our members spoke with Dr. J___, **principal** at Calumet School, his response was: "There is a great need for **tutoring classes** besides the one in the schools, because of the fast transience of youth from the inner-city schools . . ." He wants to be kept informed of our progress. Another member spoke with Mr. McC , **a dean and tutor** of Dwight D. Eisenhower High School, [who] agreed that there is a definite need for **tutoring and GED classes**, for the teen-age mothers, dropouts, and students with poor reading and writing skills . . . He also wants us to keep him abreast of our progress. (Calumet Park Covenant Church)*

Ron W___, Sheriff, sees 1) alcohol and drug abuse, and 2) vandalism as major problems in the community. Possible help for these problems includes leadership that encourages support of the law enforcement system, and programs that address the problems and encourage people to get involved. Craig M___, Agri-Business executive, sees our biggest problems as 1) decline of the middle-class farm, 2) relationships between business people and farmers and 3) drugs. Churches and social agencies need to work together with the help of specialists. (Deer Creek Presbyterian Church)

By contrast, interviews with typical residents are usually more rambling and less focused; they are more likely to tell their personal story, and to include more information than you need in a brief interview:

*Fred C___, a single parent with three children and receiving public aid, stated that due to his children he feels that something **more for children and youth** to do would be appropriate. He also stated that the churches contribute a great deal to the community, especially the Methodist Church through its food pantry. He also stated that if a need arose he would feel more comfortable approaching the Methodist Church rather than his own. (Leet Memorial United Methodist Church and Boyd's Grove United Methodist Church)*

*C.H., an interviewee from the food pantry, is 22 years old, legally separated, has two dependents and is expecting a third child. Her immediate need was **housing**. She is presently renting at $200.00/ mo. plus utilities. She served with the U.S. Army for 4 1/2 years and worked one year as a secretary. She got out of the service in January 1988. She is a lifetime resident of the area. She would like . . . [list of desired ministries]. (St. Mary's Catholic Church, Alexandria)*

Some churches use group interviews (discussions) effectively. The group stimulates participation that both gathers information and encourages support for the program. This committee interviewed participants in other church ministries:

> *We conducted one set of interviews with four parents whose chil-*
> *dren are currently enrolled in our after-school program. Because*
> *they have children, their major community concerns were for*
> ***children and youth***. *They were also concerned about having*
> *activities that would encourage moral values and keep children*
> *productive and "out-of-trouble" . . .*
>
> *We conducted two interviews with clients of the Community Food*
> *Pantry which we house in our building and support as an ecumeni-*
> *cal endeavor. They echoed the same concern about* ***education*** *. . .*
> *One woman brought along a copy of the school paper which her*
> *daughter edits,* ***but she could only show it to people because she***
> ***herself cannot read***. *(Cornell Baptist Church)*

You might want to hold a larger group interview like this community meeting that was sponsored by a group of churches to "interview the
town" and to generate interest in their project. Even people who could
not attend participated by sending letters which were read aloud and
incorporated into their summary:

> *On September 26, a Public Forum was held* ***to gather input and***
> ***help publicize the existence of the project***. *It was publicized in the*
> *local paper by the committee public relations person, in the*
> *churches and by word of mouth . . . With the combination of discus-*
> *sion and letters submitted by interested persons unable to attend,*
> *[these issues emerged]:* ***1. Quality day-care, 2. Youth center, 3.***
> ***Service for the elderly, 4. Latch-key children service, 5. Teen***
> ***volunteer program and 6. Classes to assist and inform the public***.
> *(Immaculate Conception Catholic Church)*

Since interviews create interest, your committee should find ways to
share the information you receive and the decisions you reach. Your
summaries should affirm all suggestions but push toward a focus for
your ministry:

> *As we began to search for community needs that were both* ***urgent***
> ***and manageable***, *we started by polling our own membership.*
> *Knowing that we could not address* ***all of the needs discovered***, *we*
> *narrowed our scope to three areas of ministry . . .* ***child abuse***

*, elderly care, and crisis counseling. (Hope Presbyte-
h)*

ing report, prepared by a joint committee of two urban
churches, contains the basic elements that bring ministry into focus,
namely:

— wide variety of representative interviews (in this case an
   unusually large number of people were contacted);
— general description of the community context for ministry;
— primary areas for ministry and secondary areas of concern;
— resources potentially available for ministry; and
— affirmation of the church's role in social ministry.

*An itemization of responses of 49 interviews performed by our joint
congregations is available, but here is a summary of these interviews. There were an even number of black and white, male and
female, and different age groups represented. Sixteen of the interviews were with residents who had been in the area less than 10
years while 31 were with residents of more than 10 years. We
surveyed a wide variety of professions and interest groups . . . In
general, the surveys recognize the neighborhood positively for its
general stability at this time, for the diversity of people (age, race,
economic mix), for the feelings of pride evident in certain parts of
neighborhood and for the overall quality of housing. The areas of
primary concern raised by the majority of the people interviewed
were lack of supervised activities and a community resource center
for children. This was thought to be related to the development of
gangs, loitering, problems with drugs and alcohol. The second most
commonly recognized problem in the area was crime, in part
thought to be secondary to the lack of adequate supervision after
school and on weekends. Further down on the list of priorities were
lack of adequate upkeep for properties, poor access to business and
other entertainment, and lack of adequate government support in the
area . . . There are a number of resources which are available in the
area which were frequently recognized by the interviewees. Perhaps
because church members were interviewing, local churches were
recognized as the number one potential resource for improving*

conditions in the neighborhood. (First-Meridian Heights Presbyterian Church)

Interviews rarely simplify the questions; they generally complicate your decision-making with many more options and a much more complex texture of existing conditions and probable causes. But you will come away from these encounters enriched by the discovery of new resources and energized by the need to make a start—somewhere.

Summary

Steps Three, Four, and Five combine exploration, reflection, and interviews. This direct contact with institutional leaders and typical citizens will help you gain a richer appreciation for the essential elements of program development and, equally important, a network of relationships with a broad base of people who share your concerns and your commitments to change.

Most committees enjoy this part of the study because they have a chance to express their beliefs and feelings and to explore the underside of communities they have taken for granted. You can summarize in two or three pages what you have learned in Steps Three, Four, and Five, with particular focus on the invisible people, the intangible forces, and your interviews with community people.

Choose Your Focus of Ministry

If you have the luxury of time, then your decision for ministry should be informed and solid. Some committees begin with a commitment to a particular program, and the community study confirms or shifts their direction. Other committees consider a variety of options, with each new step winnowing down the possibilities and lifting up a few viable alternatives. However you approach it, your committee should now make a preliminary decision.

Guidelines

Your task is to agree on a brief statement of focus for your new ministry. This statement must be clear enough for other people to see the possibilities and yet remain as an initial draft to be shaped with the participation of others. Your challenge is to articulate your goal in such a way that it can win the contentment of a much larger group.

Frequently, you are asked to state your goal in a single sentence. Although we affirm the need for simplicity and clarity, single sentence goal statements usually are so broad that they raise as many questions as they resolve. Rather, bring your ministry into focus with just enough detail to provide a basis for action.

Your goal should be specific to a particular community problem and sufficiently limited that you can accomplish it. It should be appropriate to the present time and within the capacity of the supporting groups. Others should be able to recognize its significance if they are to support its goals.

Examples from Churches

First, here are a couple of single sentence goal statements. While they are worthy goals, they are too global to be translated into specific programs and find either support or success:

> *Our mission is education for the illiterate.*
> *To work with young people between the ages of 5 and 18.*

Negative statements are another problem. A statement of goals set in the context of less desirable alternatives is awkward because it places the emphasis on what it is not:

> *There is a **complexity of problems** in this community as in most inner cities: many functionally illiterate adults, malnutrition, unemployment, scarcity of jobs needing the level of skills of this population, child abuse, drug abuse, lack of day care facilities for children and elders, teen-age pregnancy, etc. Within this context are **housing needs** [which they chose].*

On the other hand, this committee uses negative information effectively to heighten interest and challenge commitment to the ministry they are recommending:

> *Our community has undergone **great change** in the last two decades. It can now be described as predominantly Hispanic, young, and low income. Existing community institutions attempt to deal with social concerns, but with their limited resources they focus on the most severe problems in a crisis intervention style. Often, they are able to offer only band-aid solutions. **No existing community organization focuses primarily on parent and child education. The lack of this service has encouraged us to focus our project in this area.** (Douglas Park Covenant Church)*

Some committees use the interest created by their interviews as a platform for recommended ministry. This goal statement invites the support of all those interviewed, first affirming their community and then offering a program based on common goals:

In summary, people do not feel that the community is improving, but rather declining, as evidenced by more vacant lots, less housing available for low income households, few community activities for children and youth, concern for children's safety, poor achievement in school, and few jobs available. Two themes ran through the conversations:

1. People care about the quality of education and the renewal of the community, not just opportunities for themselves.
2. People are interested in finding ways to help children and youth develop into educated and productive members of society. (Cornell Baptist Church)

The following statements are focused and brief. They are specific in goal and content, yet broad enough to stimulate community support:

Our goal is to provide a continuum of care for older adults who are unable to remain alone, by drawing on the full range of our congregational and community resources. (University Park Christian Church)

The group probably most resistant to any social ministries is the group we want to target—parents with battered children . . . They have difficulty in parenting and lack identification of their needs. And they distrust help. (St. Mary's Catholic Church, Alexandria)

Summary

Every step contributes something in shaping community ministry, and the whole picture is greater than any one person's experience. As the program develops, the participants in ministry become real to one another as people under the same God with many common hopes and aspirations.

When your ministry includes both personal contact and time for reflection, together you can recognize and discuss the intangible forces both within individuals and in society, in their shared concern for both spiritual inadequacy and social injustice that become apparent in community ministries. Why should children of God feel so alienated and denied by intangible forces greater than themselves? What can we do for individual people and for the larger social causes of their personal problems? Concern for these religious and political issues is a natural consequence of sharing among caring people. We'll look at these issues more fully in subsequent chapters as we consider the identity of the congregation and the organizational structure of ministry.

For now, it is enough to find a place where ministry can make a difference to real people in the immediate community and to begin building together with new friends and allies.

PART II

Congregational Identity

Your study of the social context (Part I) develops a foundation for your community ministry. With a solid base of information and community contacts, your committee has probably become aware of the most urgent individual needs and the most dysfunctional systems. You have a good sense of where you might begin developing a social ministry and some idea about how much work may be involved.

But there is a second dimension to launching a ministry, beyond the facts of community analysis or the depth of available resources. To gain the support of your church, the ministry must touch the nerve of congregational concern and speak the language of congregational compassion. Church members will filter your facts and recommendations through their own values and commitments. Nothing is convincing that is out of sync with the character of the congregation, and few projects will find support if they are at odds with the kind of church the members believe themselves to be.

Congregational identity incorporates the beliefs and commitments that hold a congregation together, motivate its members, and make it distinctive from others. You can articulate some of these beliefs, but many commitments cannot be put into words. Sometimes they are carried quietly in rhythms of ritual and are interpreted only through stories. The church acts out these values and commitments in the patterns of church life—what the church does and how it does it.

Congregational identity, like personal character, takes its shape from the accumulation of experiences. It gives the group coherence and a basis for making decisions. Embedded in congregational identity are the criteria for what is acceptable and the sources of energy for ministry. The identity of the congregation sifts through and tests the recommendations for a social ministry, as it does with all other decisions. The decision to begin a social ministry is more than a procedural or political process: it is an important affirmation of the basic commitments we share as a community of Christians.

The next task you face, then, often goes unspoken, though it always happens in some form. To establish your social ministry, your committee will need to find the aspects of your congregation's identity that support your cause. Elements of faith will confirm that it is right to become involved with these issues, and historical precedents will give stature to the ministry you recommend.

Some committees never listen, but always talk: they try to convince the congregation with a sales pitch for their idea. We encourage you, rather, to explore the character of your congregation, looking for openings that will more naturally give your proposal a place in the active identity of the congregation. Knowing your congregational identity is both energizing and seductive. Examining history and sharing the stories that give the congregation unity and purpose will energize your committee. But some people become so fascinated by their memories that identity becomes an end in itself, distracting them from developing new ministries. Keep in mind the purpose of your explorations: to strengthen your congregation's commitments to ministries of all sorts, including your response to community needs.

Four elements of congregational identity are especially significant in supporting social ministry. The first three form a triangle of insights: from scripture, tradition, and experience. Your primary sources for this material will be church leaders and official documents. But it is important also to develop a broader base of understanding about your congregation. Therefore, we encourage you to gather information from the members through a survey.

We suggest these four steps in exploring your congregational identity:

STEP ONE: Identify Your Biblical Foundations. Although Scripture is foundational for all Christians, every church shapes its own traditional way of understanding the text. The congregation's biblical faith gives us a window that looks two ways. For the church, Scripture is a way to see the world; for identity, Scripture is a way to see the church.

STEP TWO: Find Sources in Your Church Heritage. Every congregation keeps alive selected elements from its broad Christian past and more recent denominational heritage. We trace the roots of heritage in creeds and official statements, programs and actions of the larger church, and the "saints" we share with other Christians across the years.

STEP THREE: Build on Your Congregational History. You can often predict what kinds of ministry a congregation will support, including social ministries, by looking at the ways members remember their own historical experiences. We will explore congregational history by listening for the stories of who they are as a church, how they got there, and how they have related to the community.

STEP FOUR: Analyze Your Strengths and Limitations through a Survey. You can learn a great deal about the values and commitments of the congregation by asking questions of a broad sample of the members. This separate source of information may both confirm and challenge what you have learned from church leaders during the other steps in your identity study.

Identify Your Biblical Foundations

A theological tradition grounded in a biblical faith is basic to the identity of every congregation. Some churches emphasize the theological tradition carried in teaching and sacraments, but grounded in a biblical faith. Other churches put the emphasis on the individual relationship with their biblical faith, but carried in theological tradition that supports individual interpretation. In both, the Bible is central to faith traditions, and faith traditions carry their interpretation of the Bible.

Functionally, church members differ in the ways we acquire and apply our biblical foundations. We have learned the Bible in different places—from the liturgy and from Sunday school, from personal study and disciplined classes, from the pulpit and the choir. Further, personal experiences may shape the ways we use it: some of us are comfortable and some hesitant, some proclaim and some are burned out. The task for your committee is to identify your congregation's biblical tradition: how does it hear the biblical faith, and how is that faith seen to support your social ministry? For additional guidance, see *Church Doors Open Outward* by Dorothy B. Bloom (Valley Forge, PA: Judson Press, 1987).

Guidelines

Your group has access to the congregation's biblical faith in three broad areas: your assumptions, your proclamations, and your decision-making process. Your assumptions are most compelling because they show how your biblical faith has been absorbed into the thought and habits of individuals and into the patterns of congregational life. We use scripture most frequently to maintain the assumptions of faith and weave such rehearsals of faith into our church music and prayers, into the gestures and phrases we take for granted until we have forgotten the source ("God be with you" becomes "goodbye"). But important as the study of lingual and behavioral assumptions may be, it is outside the interests of most groups advocating social ministry.

More likely, you can study the proclamation of the biblical tradition as it comes from the pulpit where the text is preached and from all sorts of classes where the faith is taught, shared, and modeled. You can study sermons for content and intent—for what is said and what is assumed, for the requested response and the reaction it actually receives. You can attend classes to learn in the interaction with others who attend, discuss, decide, and act in response to questions of faith. You have endless opportunities within the church to explore what people think and believe.

You may find that decisive moments provide the acid test of the biblical tradition: on what faith foundation does the congregation decide to act? You can listen to the biblical appeals and warrants that are advanced in the discussion when your congregation makes a decision. You may listen to the rationale the members offer and read how they explain the decisions they have made. For our reflections here, we review several basic themes that churches use to explain their decisions to engage in social ministry.

The way the congregation reads the Bible tells them about the text; it also tells the committee about the church. By listening carefully, your committee will be able to find the themes of biblical faith that are important to your congregations. These themes may not be systematic like a theological text; diverse—even contradictory—views are often carried comfortably in the same congregation.

Examples from Churches

Most congregations anchor their social ministries in a familiar text like Luke 4:18-19, where Jesus begins his ministry by reading from Isaiah in the synagogue, or Matthew 25:31ff., where the Son of Man judges the nations according to those who cared for "the least of these who are members of my family." But congregations use these texts (and others) differently, and those differences guide their ministries and reflect their unique styles. In reviewing their biblical foundations for social ministry, we find several themes running through congregational materials. Your committee may recognize one or more of these themes in your own congregation's biblical tradition, and you may find other interpretations that stimulate their support for social ministry.

> —*We have been **called by God** to respond to God's love by our concern for **creation** or our sharing of **salvation**.*
> —*We are **responsible and obedient** to God's law and justice, sometimes to **serve those in need** and sometimes to **challenge and change** the evil we find.*
> —*We talk of **God's presence** in and among us through images of Spirit, Jesus, Body of Christ, and Kingdom of God.*

"We Have Been Called by God . . ."

Christians—Protestants and Catholics alike—feel called by God to engage in social ministry; it is more than just a personal or rational decision. In a classic comparison, a Protestant church feels the call from the biblical text, while a Catholic parish feels rooted in its sacramental sense of calling:

> *In the New Testament Christ **calls to us** in Matthew 7:12: "Do for others what you want them to do for you," and in Matthew 5:14-16 we are called into the wider community. (Community United Church of Christ)*

> ***By our Baptism we have been called** to be disciples and to go and preach the Good News of Jesus. How better to do this than by actions that prove our love for the brokenhearted, the downtrodden and the rejected! (Luke 4: 18-19) (St. Mary's Catholic Church, Indianapolis)*

Some congregations hear God calling them to develop and maintain creation; others explicitly reject humanitarian reasons in order to emphasize God's initiative. Although theologians have suggested that these views conflict, we find that either one can motivate a church for social ministry, and some churches affirm both. Compare these two excerpts:

> *In Matthew 25:31-46 we are called to service in the name of Our Lord Jesus Christ. Every Sunday in our bulletin we read "Enter to*

*Worship—Depart to Serve." We are reminded that worship of God does not only take place in church on Sunday, but that we **worship God by serving throughout creation.** (Avondale Presbyterian Church)*

*Our church has never been involved in its community for "humanitarian" reasons . . . [but rather for] our understanding of individual and corporate salvation . . . For us, salvation is more than being "saved from hell" ; it is an experience that transforms all of life's priorities, loyalties, behaviors, and relationships. Therefore, **our salvation,** rather than allowing us to selfishly enjoy or hoard our experience with Christ, **calls us to be involved in our world and to share this salvation with our community.** (Cornell Baptist Church)*

In responding to God's call, we can be transformed. In this joint statement, two cooperating churches say that social ministry can lift them from self-centered activities and allow them to use their theological differences constructively:

*"Do nothing from selfishness or conceit, but in humility count others better than yourselves. Let each of you look not only to his own interests, but also the interests of others." (Phil. 2: 3-4) . . . Our members recognize that the desire for **personal salvation without social redemption is not only selfish but impossible** . . . We have conservative and progressive members enabling our churches to live in a **"dynamic middle" rather than a "dead center."** (First-Meridian Heights Presbyterian Church)*

"We Are Responsible and Obedient to God . . ."

The commanding character of biblical passages is a relief to some church members. It is important to this committee that they have willingly responded to God's expectations of them:

*Jesus spelled out our **responsibility as individuals and as a church** in Matthew: 25:31-46. It was in these verses that he said: "Come, oh blessed of my Father, inherit the kingdom prepared for you from the foundation of the world; for I was hungry and you gave me food,*

*I was thirsty and you gave me drink, I was a stranger and you
welcomed me, I was naked and you clothed me, I was sick and you
visited me, I was in prison and you came to me." (Riverside Park
United Methodist Church)*

Whether by call or by obedience, congregations engaged in prophetic ministries see God as the source of authority. They do not act on
their own, but God expects them to change the social order, as these two
churches announce:

*Generally the poor are oppressed and locked out of the mainstream
of our society . . . God is calling us to open up opportunities to all
who, as the Bible states, "Knock, Seek, Look." **The Bible tells us
we fight not against flesh and blood, but against evil rulers who
seek through sin of pride and greed to keep others on the outside
looking in.** (Calumet Park Covenant Church)*

*If war be sin, we believe that we are called to abolish war, for we
. . . seek to listen **obediently to Jesus** . . . "Blessed are the Peace-
makers, for they shall be called the children of God." (Matt. 5.9) . . .
Peace-making, for the Brethren, is . . . assertively seeking reconciliation and compassionate justice. (Manchester Church of the
Brethren)*

"We Know God Is Present with Us . . ."

Many churches recall how they have experienced God's presence with
them in their ministries, but they use quite different images: Spirit, Jesus,
Body of Christ, Kingdom of God, and an appeal to actions as more
honest than words. This committee finds comfort in the Spirit of God's
presence in every circumstance:

*God not only created time, place, and us, but he is involved with us
. . . If it seems that our task is much too great for us . . . we are
assured by the word that the Lord will be with us and that He is our
strength. As found in Zechariah 4:6 "Not by might nor by power,
but **by my Spirit,** says the Lord of Hosts." (First Presbyterian
Church, Canton)*

For some groups, God is present in the person of Jesus:

*The church **looks to Jesus** in his relationship with the community. We **look to Jesus** for the specific directions that he has given, to love our Father with our heart, mind, soul, and strength, and to love our neighbors as ourselves. (First Presbyterian Church, Canton)*

Some congregations emphasize their identity as the Body of Christ, continuing his ministry:

*If we take the analogy of Paul concerning the church as the **body of Christ** seriously then we realize we dare not leave those who suffer in any way to their own devices and resources either. For we in many ways are **His only hands, His only feet, and His only voice.** (Leet Memorial United Methodist Church and Boyd's Grove United Methodist Church)*

The Kingdom of God has energized believers since the ministry of Jesus, and it still has broad spiritual, social, and sometimes political significance:

***God's great compassion, or the Kingdom,** has three aspects, inner, beyond, and historical . . . Our understanding of the call to social ministry is founded on this perception of the Kingdom, where the operating dynamic is love, and the character is peace and justice. **The church is attempting to give its community a glimpse of this Kingdom.** (Edwin Ray United Methodist Church)*

An arrogant, condescending attitude can infect ministries where church members come to feel that they alone have something to offer. Aware of this risk, some congregations acknowledge that they learn and gain from social ministries. In caring for others, they themselves are healed; in sharing their faith, they find Christ already in the lives of the people with whom they work:

*An important basis for social ministry is to affirm that . . . **all people are loved by God** . . . The dignity and uniqueness of every individual, the equality of all peoples, and our partnership in this life*

*and on this world, all open us to **acquaint ourselves with our
neighbors, share in their struggles and their pain, and learn from
them.*** *(South Chicago Covenant Church)*

Some congregations act out their biblical faith more than they
express it in the language of theology. They prefer to point to their
actions rather than articulate their faith:

*We are not a posturing church. We **let our deeds do the talking.**
We are forever mindful that we are God's hands and feet on earth.
**We don't have to be God's mouth. We strive humbly to love by
serving, to teach by doing, and to preach by being.** That is our
theology. (Millard Congregational United Church of Christ)*

Despite the centrality of preaching for Pentecostal groups, the
committee members at this Spirit-filled congregation sum up their faith
simply:

*Our church also follows a covenant which instructs us to be **mindful
of how we walk, talk, and are seen by the world.** We are the salt of
the earth and a city that is placed on a hill that cannot be hid.
Therefore we know that we must support missions abroad but never
forget to impact our immediate community. (Sweet Holy Spirit
Baptist Church)*

Summary

Once you have settled on your sources, you should be able to identify the
language and style of biblical tradition that pastors and members find
persuasive. When you recognize the channels they are using, you can
formulate your ministry in a way they will understand. Often in this
exercise you need to discover the negative values of the church—what
doesn't communicate—as much as what does. You may find that your
church emphasizes creation or salvation, or embraces both. Some of the
members of your church may want to respond to God's call in their
freedom, and others may want the authority to feel they are commanded
to respond. All churches feel the presence of God, but some images of
presence fit more comfortably in your congregational tradition than
others.

STEP TWO

Find Sources in Your Church Heritage

Heritage provides the bridge between the timeless sources of faith, such as the Bible and the sacraments, and the particular experiences of faith-fulness among the members of a congregation. It supports social minis-try with a framework of values and commitments that are larger and older than the congregation itself. The affirmation of social ministry within that framework makes a program legitimate in the eyes of the local church; if we cannot show that affirmation, the program will remain suspect.

Church heritage is different from congregational history. History is what the congregation remembers from its own past. Heritage embraces a larger framing of the Christian faith, including the traditions and feelings that accrue to a congregation simply by belonging to a wider gathering of churches in the flow of Christian experience. History is the memory of the congregation, while heritage is the faith tradition they carry, which also carries them.

Guidelines

We find church heritage in many sources. We see it in official faith statements and policy papers and in church-wide patterns of organization and decision making. Names carry theological traditions—Baptist, Evangelical, Reformed, Unitarian-Universalist. Historic figures like Augustine, Aquinas, Luther, Calvin, and Wesley still impact our think-ing. We can look at our architecture, examine our liturgy, listen to our music, read our creeds, observe our rituals, and talk with our historians— and yet heritage is always more intangible than any simple factual summary.

With this wealth of material available, you need to focus your search for sources of support for your ministry to make your study manageable. I suggest that you begin with the objective, official statements and move toward the more particular, personal stories. Your denomination's policy statements in areas that relate to your proposed ministry will be fairly accessible. Beyond those documents, I encourage you to look for ministries or actions of your wider church group that offer precedents (both structural and motivational) for your congregation to support your proposed program. Finally, we urge you to explore the stories of people in your own communion who have carried the faith in action and who symbolize the best of who you are.

Include three components, then, in your study of your church heritage: (a) examine church creeds and policy statements, (b) look for precedents in previous ministries, and (c) find the "saints" of the church.

Examples from Churches:
Church Creeds and Policy Statements

Official church statements give permission and encouragement for local congregations to become involved in social ministry. The documents provide a tangible link between the issues facing the congregation and the social traditions of the church. A Methodist church takes pride in its pioneering church policy:

> *In 1910, the Methodist Church became the first denomination to draft a social creed in which we find these words: "We believe in the right and duty of persons to work for . . . the elimination of economic and social distress." (Leet Memorial United Methodist Church and Boyd's Grove United Methodist Church)*

Catholic parishes often cite the more recent pastoral epistles of the United States Conference of Bishops:

> *In the recent US Bishops' pastoral entitled "Economic Justice for All," we see expressed the heart of the Church in its option for the poor: "We feel the pain of our sisters and brothers who are poor, unemployed, homeless, living on the edge—it summons the Church*

*also to be an instrument in assisting people to experience the
liberating power of God in their own lives, so that they may respond
to the gospel in freedom and dignity." (St. Joan of Arc Catholic
Church)*

Although these historic statements may help when you need board
approval, fund raising, or other official sanctions, most congregations use
official statements sparingly or not at all. To gain wide support for the
ministry among your parishioners, the other, less formal elements of
heritage will be more powerful.

Examples from Churches:
Precedents in Previous Ministries

Planning committees often find support for community ministries by
citing previous activities and continuing programs that document their
denominational commitment to social ministry. Typically a Methodist
church will trace its roots back to ministries among working class people
in England and the United States:

> *Early Methodists developed schools, clinics, programs for the aged,
> and even cottage industries for unemployed. Their view of Christian
> discipleship called for giving food to the hungry, clothing to the
> naked, visiting or helping those sick or in prison. **This tendency
> continues** in the American Church. (Irvington United Methodist
> Church)*

The Church of the Brethren, the Mennonites, and other pietist
movements have a particular historical consciousness carried by—and
carrying—a community with distinctive faith commitments. In choosing
a pacifist interpretation of the Gospel, they align themselves with people
who are persecuted and pushed to the margins of society. This Brethren
church is well aware of its heritage as a basis for social ministry:

> *Persecution in Europe resulted in many members migrating to
> America from 1719 to 1729 in search of religious and economic
> freedom. The Brethren **refused to serve in the Revolutionary War**
> and moved further into the wilderness including Maryland and*

*Virginia. There they gained their livelihood from the soil, **lived at***
***peace with the Indians**, and established new churches.*
At the time of the Civil War the Brethren lived in both the North and
South. Some draftees served, others hired substitutes or sought
asylum in the North or in Free Territory. Others sought to reconcile
*differences, resulting in **persecution, economic hardship, and***
***martyrdom**. **Conscientious objectors** were sent to prison or granted*
a noncombatant status during WWI. Alternative service was an
additional option during WWII . . . As an historical peace church,
*these **convictions have led members into worldwide ventures and***
***volunteer service** for promoting peace. (Lafayette Church of the*
Brethren)

For most congregations, denominational heritage is not constricting
but liberating as a basic platform on which to build community outreach
programs. As you work through this study, you are laying a foundation
that moves from policies to ministries—from the abstractions of faith
statements to the embodiment of faith actions.

Examples from Churches:

"Saints" of the Church

Planning committees in Catholic parishes rarely use the precedent of
church-wide ministry programs to claim their heritage of social ministry.
Most often they use the lives of saints. For Catholics there are always
stories and events around individuals who embody the caring qualities of
the faith. This church's statement is typical of many:

There are many stories of countless numbers of saints who have
*given and helped the needy and the poor. **St. Vincent DePaul** is one*
known to many for his quiet way of knocking on the door of the
poor, offering them help here and now, and then leaving silently . . .
No fuss, no muss, no embarrassing questions or case number, just
*help, share, and love unselfishly. **Pope Gregory** was another person*
in our heritage who urged and brought about . . . land reforms for
the more humane treatment of servants and tenant farmers . . .
***Mother Teresa of Calcutta**, known all over the world today, speaks*

and demonstrates the attitudes of social caring and sharing we as a church wish to express. (St. Mary's Catholic Church, Alexandria).

Often the name of their own parish embodies their identity. This city church has been working toward a ministry with youth:

Our name-saint, Joan of Arc, was a simple peasant girl who was "of the people," rather than "of the organization." She was a champion of the "Will of God." She was a woman of action; she held a grand disdain for obstacles whether, major or minor, that blocked her path . . . Joan was youth. She was scarcely 18 when she raised the siege of Orleans. Joan is youth. Joan, the maid, remains with us today as a model of courage and maidenly virtue in a world so much in need of her example. (St. Joan of Arc Catholic Church)

Some Protestants also find a sense of Christian caring embodied in the name of a congregation:

When the United Brethren and Evangelical United Brethren Church combined, they renamed themselves St. Luke's Evangelical United Brethren Church. There are two implications in the name they selected. First, St. Luke was a physician—a loving and caring person who helped others. Secondly, United Brethren implies a group of people joining together to help their fellow man (brethren). Social concern and ministry could therefore be considered a natural extension of St. Luke's name.

Although the Protestant Reformation made a theological point of denying the saints, contemporary Protestants readily name heroic figures who embody their beliefs. When asked to identify "a symbolic leader of your faith who has influenced you in developing social ministries," the church leaders we work with most frequently point to Martin Luther King, Jr., and Pope John XXIII.

In addition, each Protestant denomination can name champions who have made an impact within that communion, but who rarely find much following outside. This Protestant pantheon tends to include significant theological leaders who have emerged at an important juncture in the life of the church. Catholics, on the other hand, rarely confuse the wisdom of theologians with the piety of saints.

In their search for identity, Presbyterians turn first to the Swiss theologian-reformer John Calvin and American pastor-patriot John Witherspoon:

> *John Calvin not only preached the gospel of salvation, but a gospel of social responsibility . . . John Witherspoon signed the Declaration of Independence as his ministerial commitment to justice and freedom . . . Our history is replete with persons who have been on the frontiers of all major social issues. (Hope Presbyterian Church)*

Baptist churches find a spiritual ancestor in the early American fight for religious freedom by Roger Williams and in a theologian-activist from the turn of the century:

> *Walter Rauschenbusch is credited by some to be among the first proponents of the social gospel. As a Baptist pastor in New York's "Hell's Kitchen" in the late nineteenth century, Rauschenbusch saw the need . . . for better housing, better working conditions, and the elimination of disease and crime. (Baptist Temple)*

Summary

You may find the key to locating the saints of the church in the way the Methodists treat the Wesleys. Every Methodist church seems to remember their founders, but each for a different reason—according to their own situation. For example, a church in a rural town recalls how they preached "the Good News in small towns and rural areas like ours," while a more urban congregation with a strong educational program remembers that John Wesley "founded schools because he realized the importance of education." You cannot simply mold the lives of great leaders to fit the needs of a local situation, but the giants of the faith offer a rich variety of stories of commitment for us to draw upon as we shape our ministries. In drawing on past saints, you suggest a longevity of commitment to ministry, which you invite the present membership to continue.

Build on Your Congregational History

History is not the dead past, but the strengths and softness, the confidence and weakness, the heroes and the hidden bodies that a congregation carries from previous experience. There are many sources for such history. Creeds might be described as the resolution of former theological disputes, and rituals re-enact once controversial decisions about faith, authority, and the meaning of membership in this congregation. The architecture, pictures, and symbols that adorn the church offer public witness to the historic identity of the congregation. The hymns and special music, the prayers and liturgy, the offering received and the sacraments celebrated, the announcements and rubrics of worship, the roles of clergy and laity—all are elements of the congregation's history enacted in the present. Congregational history is everywhere and inescapable.

Church stories, however, are the most accessible carriers of history. We are interested in the stories of people and events that are remembered and shared in congregational life. Sometimes you hear these stories in formal situations, but more likely you relate them in conversation—like gossip—when humorous memories carry hard values that strengthen membership commitments. These stories also surface in a decision-making crisis, providing models for choices and energy for sealing the choice with action. For further reading in this approach, see *Transforming a People of God* by Denham Grierson (Melbourne: Joint Board of Christian Education, 1984).

The stories live because they show us what is authentic in the congregation. Sometimes they guide us like a rudder through hard times. Often they confirm a sense of belonging—for those who tell them and those who listen. Stories help us incorporate outsiders who want to join the church, as we invite them to listen and to add a story of their own. Stories may be used for discipline and guidance, recalling the past to affirm or challenge the beliefs or behavior of the present. For the purpose of this study, we will look at the stories that connect the congregation with prior experiences in social ministry.

Guidelines

Listen for the stories that the congregation remembers and retells. For many members, especially the older ones, these are the foundations on which the church is built. They are retold at celebrations, in times of decision, in moments of consolation, and in other transitional experiences. We recount these memories of significant events and people to give ballast and direction to congregational identity in moments of uncertainty and change. These stories bring a variety of emotions—humor for their human failings, anger for decisions that now inhibit our choices, reverence for sacrifice in behalf of lofty ideals, and commitment to maintain a continuity with their remembered greatness.

As your committee seeks to mobilize your congregation for social ministry, collect your significant stories: who are you as a church, how did you get there, and how do you relate to your community?

In our experience, church histories cluster around characteristic themes. We have found five themes in the stories churches tell about their histories in community context, and these images are useful in mobilizing congregations for a style of ministry that fits their historic identity. We have previously reported these images in materials published by The Alban Institute and Westminster/John Knox Press (see bibliography). You should not force your stories through any prescribed theme or design, but look for the images that reflect congregational identity and therefore mobilize the energy of your congregation.

As examples of the way focused images can mobilize churches, we clustered these mini-stories around five basic themes by which congregations link their histories to social ministries:

- Journey stories of ethnic-cultural congregations;
- Crisis stories of churches that struggle for survival;
- Rooted stories with a place for spiritual growth;
- Service stories of caring for people; and
- Mission stories of vision for a better world.

Examples from Churches:
Journey Stories of Ethnic-Cultural Congregations

The earliest memories have roots in other countries, most frequently the old European nations. Sometimes these are told from the perspective of those who came and sometimes from the viewpoint of those who welcomed the newcomer. The first example comes from an Hispanic congregation that remembers two previous waves of migration. In these few words they project their own experiences into previous generations ("We've always been this way") and tell a story their denomination also finds appealing:

> *From its inception our church was **an oasis welcoming those people whom other established churches were reluctant to accept into their fold.** The early membership consisted of the newly arrived **Bohemians** who did not fit the requirements of the existing local churches. Later on it consisted of displaced **Appalachian whites** who were attracted by the social gospel preached and practiced even in those early years. We acted in accordance with the teachings of Jesus, striving to meet successfully the test of true fellowship. (Millard Congregational United Church of Christ)*

This church makes an explicit connection between the challenges of the past and the ministry they are now developing:

> *From the very beginning, education of their children was of concern to the parents in the immigrant section. The first call to a permanent pastor stipulated that **he should conduct a school** . . . Education [was] the church's focus for the next half-century, with a sensitivity to the new families who arrived **jobless, homeless, and rootless** . . . In the 1960's, our community ethnic composition changed as Hispanics became the predominant group. In 1972 the Spanish ministry began . . . with an **emphasis on education.** (Douglas Park Covenant Church)*

Two Lutheran churches, one Anglo and one Chinese, weave their stories together as they plan a shared ministry of education and employment for recent Chinese immigrants:

*The early Immanuel Lutheran Church ministered to a congregation of Swedish immigrants who found themselves in **straitened circumstances**. They lived in shanties or in other crowded rented dwellings . . . A cholera epidemic in 1854 and a failure of most banks added to their privations. Through all of this the church helped its members **find jobs, learn the language, and adapt to the culture** and surroundings of their new homeland. (Immanuel Lutheran Church)*

*Many of the Chinese Church congregation endured long and dangerous pilgrimages to freedom in this country. Their stories of the **hardships parallel those of Immanuel's early members**. The Chinese Church's ministry to the spiritual and social needs of today's immigrants is repeating Immanuel's early ministry to the Swedish immigrants. (Lutheran Chinese Christian Church)*

Examples from Churches:
Crisis Stories of Churches That Struggle for Survival

An even more common theme in congregational history revolves around hardship and struggle. In many ways the hard times may be more useful than the comfortable experiences. In these challenges we test our values and commitments—the stuff that gives us our identity and keeps us together when the pressure is less severe. For many congregations the memories of the crises they have survived nourish the muscle of their faith.

Some churches have memories of oppression, survival, and acceptance that set the stage for ministries with other newcomers today. This brief but poignant comment from a comparatively wealthy Catholic parish reminds the congregation of their history:

*The **Ku Klux Klan** was active in Indiana in the 20's. Catholic and foreign-born families often felt unwelcome in the inner city. **They found comfort under the wing of St. Joan of Arc Church.** (St. Joan of Arc Catholic Church)*

The memory of financial struggles often shapes the character of the church. Churches can use their stories of hardship and commitment to reclaim their character and mobilize their energies for ministry a generation later:

> _From the beginning funding was a struggle. A tithing band, projects by the women such as weekly peanut sales, kept the church afloat. When the depression of the 1930's came the church was literally **saved from bankruptcy by a few families** who mortgaged their homes to get cash to make payments on the debt . . . [During this time the **church began] an early and centering ministry in the Marion County Children's Guardian Home**. Church women provided Christmas gifts, furnished supplies, mended clothing, and taught a church school class. The church still provides similar support. (Irvington United Methodist Church)_

Another congregation names its decades by the nature of the struggle in which the church is engaged. This story is unusually frank about the gains and losses in their struggle for survival:

> _The first ten years in the life of this congregation, as expressed by those who know it best, is described as a **"Decade in the Desert"** .. "Years of Yearning". . . . The young struggling congregation moved from a bus garage to an American Legion Post to a funeral home to a borrowed apostolic church. **Even then, however, this people of God had dreams and visions** . . ._
>
> _The arrival of Reverend Fisher marked the beginning of the next decade in our history. He found the situation very bleak. The membership, which was never very large, had dwindled; the notes of more than $900.00 per month were due and the church was over $90,000 in debt. This overwhelming indebtedness, more than anything else, shaped this period labeled **"Decade of Debt."** Current members from this era still speak of fish fries, chicken dinners, the devil's funeral, and other lucrative and not so lucrative enterprises . . . All energy, so it seemed, was spent on fund-raising; but **the people had a mind to work** . . ._
>
> _The decade ended with the church debt free and with a membership on roll of nearly 400 people . . . **In the battle against the debt, many casualties occurred**. Relationships were strained, families were divided, members left and members became inactive, but the_

*church moved on. The two years following the mortgage burning were years of celebration and transition. **The people were pausing to catch their breath**. (Martin Temple A.M.E. Zion Church)*

Sometimes deep emotions create a significant gap between the historical events and congregational memories. This African-American congregation tells a vivid story of their racial transition. While the facts are inaccurate, the character of their memory is a powerful and sad reality:

*As the white flight accelerated, members left the Church never to come back. Most members moved out of the neighborhood. As membership was decreasing the black members noticed it and saw no alternative but to **try and buy the Church** . . . After a bitter struggle, **the black members were successful** in purchasing the Church. **The white members took all the funds and records**, and left the Church with a mortgage, two Pastors, and seven black members. "It was like a rapture had taken place," stated one of the members who witnessed the ordeal. (Zion Community Church)**

Although the twisting of historical facts in such a story needs to be challenged (for example, no records were lost, no property sold), it demonstrates the power of memory to shape identity and mobilize energy; it also reminds us to confirm the historical basis for the stories we tell.

Examples from Churches:
Rooted Stories with a Place for Spiritual Growth

Many churches root their identity in rich memories of places where they have experienced significant events. Place and memory are attached, and congregations will sacrifice mightily to have a space they can call their own:

[When the church] outgrew her previous location, regardless of the existing financial situation we were able to acquire a new church on

---

*Pseudonym for a church that has since withdrawn from the Project.

> *West 103rd Street. This "renovated storefront **building**" was*
> *certainly a **blessing** regardless of the problems therein. We needed*
> *a roof, a furnace and so much more but **with prayer and faith**,*
> *along with the **faithful contributions** of the people, God did just*
> *what he said he would do! (Sweet Holy Spirit)*

Some churches see their buildings as more than just a shelter for the
congregation; they also offer it as a home for a variety of community
activities. These groups find strength both in claiming their space and in
offering it to others. These congregations have no sharp line between
church members and community residents; they have a parish sense of
ministry:

> *For well over 125 years our congregation functioned as a non-*
> *denominational community church, and **the sense of being "com-***
> ***munity" remains extremely strong**. Our founders established a*
> *place for people in the community to meet and share their faith as*
> *well as their sense of mission . . . In providing a **home for our faith**,*
> *we are also providing a place for the **expression of that faith***
> ***through service** and availability to the wider community. (Commu-*
> *nity United Church of Christ)*

Examples from Churches:
Service Stories of Caring for People

One virtually universal story retells the way members care for other
members in times of danger, hardship, illness, and transitions of all sorts.
These memories tend to take two very different forms, which have a
significant impact on the development of social ministry. In the first
story the church takes pride in the way it looks after its own people:

> *We have no record of organized charities in the beginning, but there*
> *must have been the usual **"rectory door" variety**. Sewing circles*
> *made not only **baptismal gowns** and first Communion dresses, but*
> *also **clothing and bedding for the poor**. Women's Club and Legion*
> *of Mary members **visited the sick and assisted families in time of***
> ***bereavement**. These works were, however, primarily within the*
> *parish membership. (St. Joan of Arc Catholic Church)*

The other story reflects a concern for others beyond the membership of the church. By carrying such a memory, this church more easily accepts a ministry beyond present membership and more quickly joins with other churches in developing that ministry. Note also how the memory serves to reinforce in their congregational identity that "we've always done" these things:

> *The congregation **has always been evangelistic as well as mission minded**. Truck loads of corn have been sent for CROP as well as rabbits and chickens to migrant farmworkers' camps in the area. During the twenties and thirties the women canned fruit and the youth gathered canned goods, soap, towels, wash clothes, tooth brushes and paste for the Methodist Hospital in Peoria. (Leet Memorial United Methodist Church and Boyd's Grove United Methodist Church)*

Some churches look not only to the past, but also to the future, seeing service as a new story in which they themselves can be changed even as they reach out to help others:

> *It is very difficult and a very slow process to get people once again **revitalized and re-motivated**. This is why [a ministry project] is so important to us. We **need a project of social outreach**, a program in which we can reach out to each other and to the community and become an **ecumenical source of hope to all people** in this small community. (St. Mary's Catholic Church, Alexandria)*

Examples from Churches:
Mission Stories of Vision for a Better World

Some congregations look back on a history of addressing broad community problems. They seek to work with the larger institutional systems that affect the lives of everyone, and they try to change the causes of the problems people face. This church group recalls a strategy of moving from contact to awareness, from providing services to making policy:

> *In 1980 the church divided the neighborhood into seven districts, assigning an elder and deacon to each district. They were **respon-***

sible for keeping tabs on community activities and events: illness, deaths, etc. of neighborhood residents as well as church members . . . Since that time we have developed a food pantry, English classes for Asian refugees, monthly rummage sales, a summer recreation program for elementary school age children, H.O.M.E. (a house painting project), a quarterly community newsletter, and active involvement on the Boards of nearly all neighborhood multi-service centers, community, business, and ministerial associations. (Washington Street Presbyterian Church)

Congregations may find their identity in advocating and modeling innovative programs that the community might adopt and institutionalize. In the story of this church, the focus is not on the program itself but on how it influenced others:

Concern for children is characteristic of this congregation. Westminster has housed and/or sponsored a variety of programs for children, including tutoring, nursery schools, a school for gifted children of color, and a child development center for the children of migrant workers. The tutoring program later became a model for a district-wide project for the city . . . Our facility has always provided a forum and meeting place for community groups. We feel it is our opportunity to show that we believe in the unity of all God's creatures. (Westminster Presbyterian Church)

Sometimes social involvement in one era gives permission for new programs in another. From its large gothic exterior and relatively wealthy membership, you would not expect this congregation to hire a community organizer for social change—unless you knew this fragment of their story:

A century ago the Social Gospel Movement and the United Way were expressions of a common concern . . . They started prison reform, made treatment of the mentally ill more humane, began day care centers, organized programs to help immigrants make a new home in America and created public health departments and juvenile courts . . . Our church was a leader of the Social Gospel Movement. (First-Meridian Heights Presbyterian Church)

Summary

History can be your ally and resource in mobilizing your congregation for social ministry when you find precedents for commitment and when you get inside the logic of the stories the congregation tells. Enjoy your search for stories, knowing how they can help release and focus the energy of the congregation through ministry.

Analyze Your Strengths and Limitations through a Survey

We previously explored the triangle of insights that interact to shape the congregation's identity in social ministry: scripture, tradition, and experience. By now you have gathered a variety of material on your church's triangle of biblical foundations, Christian heritage, and particular history. These form the building blocks to understand how social ministry fits within your identity and to develop congregational support for your ministry.

Every few years you may wish to go the second mile beyond the leadership of the church to hear what a broadly based sample of church members thinks, feels, and believes. Your membership survey can be brief or extensive, highly focused or wide in scope, written or verbal, done individually or in groups. Whatever your method and content, as church leaders your views are likely to be generally affirmed—but you may also be surprised in several significant areas. We use a membership survey frequently because support for social ministry is an area where leaders tend to be less accurate about the beliefs and commitments of church members.

You may choose a written questionnaire that invites members to express their views within previously determined categories of response; this enables you to compare the views of members throughout your congregation. Our questionnaire covers a wide variety of information on the members' values and commitments, including questions of congregational identity, biblical faith, and the relationship between the church and its social context.

A membership survey gives you a different perspective for understanding your congregation. Much of your study of biblical foundations, church heritage, and congregational history reflects the insights and memories of church leaders, but a survey draws on a much larger base. You have summarized your work in Steps One, Two, and Three in brief narrative reports, and you may have discussed the reports with groups in the church. The survey, however, provides a statistical report and makes its impact by showing the popularity of particular views. The survey also has its limits: we may know how many people supported a particular view, but we do not know how important the question is to them. The survey gives extensive, measured information, and the narrative gives more depth and a focused intensity.

Guidelines

We suggest you plan your survey well in advance of the time you would like to share the results. Several excellent church membership surveys are available from denominational offices, seminaries, and consultants. You can design your own survey from existing material, such as the questionnaire that is published in the appendix of the *Handbook for Congregational Studies*, edited by Jackson W. Carroll, et al. (Nashville: Abingdon Press, 1986).

Your survey offers a larger framework for understanding the personal commitments and social dynamics of congregational life. As such it will help you to look first at the profile of a single congregation and then compare your results with information from other congregations. Ideally, the most stimulating educational environment for learning from a survey is a group of churches that use the same questionnaire and then discuss the results together.

Of the extensive information you can gain about your members' perspectives and the dynamics of your church, here we focus on some of the kinds of information you can learn about your congregational identity. I have organized the examples from churches around several basic questions that may concern you as you seek support and commitment for your social ministry program:

— Context: What is the relationship of the church to its
   community?
— Identity: What is the members' sense of congregational unity?
— Trust: How have members responded to our decision making?
— Faith: Does the faith of this church support this ministry?

— Commitment: Will the members give to support this ministry?
— Advocacy: Are justice issues included in this ministry?

Examples from Churches:
Context

The social sensitivity of a few leaders guides most congregations. They have little information about the way the majority of members feel about the church and even less about how they are seen in the community. Thus churches seize upon the information that helps a congregation see itself in relation to its community, as this church reports:

> *We are seen in our community as ecumenical, "open," liberal, community-minded, autonomous, tolerant, and cooperative. We see ourselves as a caring and committed community of Christians, seeking to follow the call to mission in a variety of styles and programs. (Community United Church of Christ)*

Another church discovered a genuine liability in the congregation's efforts to develop an educational outreach by church volunteers working with community people:

> *The education of the average member may make it difficult to relate effectively with the very people with whom the project seeks to work . . . [However] the education of the congregation does indicate an interest in education which suggests that an issue related to education would be supported. (First-Meridian Heights Presbyterian Church)*

This church discovered the same distance between congregation and community, but converted the gap into an opportunity:

> *Although North Church prides itself on diversity of opinion, theology, and interests, it has become evident through the membership survey that we are very homogeneous in regards to race, educational level, and to a slightly lesser degree socio-economic status. Thus, we have a great deal to learn from our community. (North United Methodist Church)*

Examples from Churches:
Identity

Since most congregational leaders emphasize the familial images of the church as "home" and the members as "family," they are often shocked to discover that many members see the church quite differently. Members in this church feel themselves to be religious without a need for intimacy; they see the church as a gathering of caring individuals, loosely knit but ready to help when needed:

> *Personal, individual religion is our focus; 78% pray every day . . .*
> *But, this personal, individual style of religion results in a low sense*
> *of church family; 38% have no close friends in the congregation . . .*
> *The membership thus seems **to work better together as individuals***
> ***than as groups.** (Baptist Temple)*

This church also recognizes the loss of the family image, but sees in mutual help an opportunity for unity:

> *We are not so much a family at this time as we are a mini-commu-*
> *nity, a more loosely knit association of individuals and groups . . .*
> *[in which] we overwhelmingly agree (83%) that our **members help***
> ***each other out in times of trouble.** (First Presbyterian Church,*
> *Canton)*

A survey can help us discover diversity within the congregation. Finding these subgroups among us may be a difficult experience; some discoveries confirm our fears, while others offer unexpected opportunity:

> *We are now aware that there is a **definite subgroup** in the congre-*
> *gation that **will not be cooperative and speaks strongly against the***
> ***project.** (St. Mary's Catholic Church, Indianapolis)*

> *We identified a **surprising sub-group** within our congregation . . .*
> *[that] believe in the local community and are **willing to give their***
> ***money to support the church** . . . We will have to make a specific*
> *effort to personally reach out to this sub-group to involve them in*
> *our ministry project. (St. Boniface Catholic Church)*

Examples from Churches:
Trust

Your committee can learn a good deal from survey questions in which members comment on congregational goals, conflicts, and decision making. For this group, the survey shows a general affirmation of their decision making but suggests an area for future concern:

> *The membership survey tends to **validate the process we employed** to arrive at a decision concerning our ministry project. It also **validates what we thought the home meetings revealed** about our corporate personality, about our understanding of the worship/ mission relationship, and about our willingness to be involved in social ministry . . . **On the other hand . . . it may be somewhat difficult for us to relinquish some of the control** over the project and to give our partners as much flexibility as they may need. (Hope Presbyterian Church)*

Examples from Churches:
Faith

Many church leaders find that in order to challenge the congregation to respond to community needs they must draw on the faith commitments of members who have little available time. This urban parish puts into words what many others have said, thought, and prayed:

> *The surveyed members answered that they perceived their church as being involved in activities of social services, but half responded that **they had no time to assist in such services.** Sixty-nine percent indicated that the pastor speaks . . . on the need to be involved in social outreach. Apparently **what is heard by the congregation does not move them to action.** The congregation sees itself as a fairly religious group and this was supported by other data . . . So the potential for giving and sharing is there in the congregation. **How to unleash that powerful action is the challenge.** (St. Mary's Catholic Church, Indianapolis)*

If congregational leaders believe they are more concerned about the community than the average church member, the results of a survey may be surprising. The survey allows many new voices to speak out, sometimes from neglected corners of the congregation:

> *The survey reports that St. Joan Church is, indeed, **motivated and inspired by its Catholic-Christian Faith to work for social outreach**. Seventy-four percent of our congregation said that their faith makes them want to work to eliminate injustice, poverty and hunger. Thirty-nine percent said they volunteer in community ministries once a month or more. (St. Joan of Arc Catholic Church)*

Examples from Churches:
Commitment

Most churches face a clear gap between the members' faith commitments and their actual involvement in ministry. This congregation combined their discoveries of a problem and their strategy for response:

> *The implications of these responses are twofold: First, we need to **design the volunteer roles in our project so that people in the parish believe that they have the time and talent to do them;** and second, given that most of our parishioners attend Sunday Worship, **we need to incorporate aspects of our ministry project in the Worship Services,** highlighting the importance of this ministry and the need for the parishioners to get involved in it. If our parish clergy promote it, our members will respond. (St. Thomas Aquinas Catholic Church)*

Through a survey your committee can assess the mood of the congregation—how it feels about itself and how the new ministry may fit into the faith and life of the membership. This church weaves faith and feelings together to help members gain strength from developing a program to improve their community:

> *From the membership survey, we learned that **we bring many strengths** to a potential project. Our congregation has a very **high morale and positive outlook** for the community's future. There is a*

> *strong sense of identification with our present community minis-*
> *tries . . . Eighty-three percent of the respondents agreed that volun-*
> *teering to help others is an expression of faith, and 74% said that*
> *their faith makes them want to eliminate poverty and hunger. [In*
> *fact] 30% already volunteer in our community ministries. (Wash-*
> *ington Street Presbyterian Church)*

Examples from Churches:

Advocacy

Perhaps the most difficult discussions (and decisions) about social
ministries arise from the conflict between those who want to provide
ministries of service to people in need and those who want to undertake
justice ministries for systemic change. A membership survey cannot
resolve the question, but it will map the terrain for you, making the
challenge very clear:

> *[Congregational values and] leadership roles tend to be **more in***
> ***the areas of finance, education, and the social life** of the parish,*
> *than in mission and social justice. (St. Mary's Catholic Church,*
> *Alexandria)*

However, in some congregations you will find strong support for
ministries that care about people and that are committed to changing
unjust conditions:

> *We understand that since we worship a God of justice, we should try*
> *to be just in our daily lives. **Programs to help the needy were***
> ***ranked equally with worship** as the highest priority for our church.*
> *(Washington Street Presbyterian Church)*

Finally, this example shows the challenge a Catholic parish finds in
its membership survey and the way it uses the strengths of Christian
identity, weaving together the elements of history, tradition, and biblical
faith into a more meaningful social ministry:

> *Finally in examining identity, 29% indicated that the Church should*

work for "Justice" by working to end inequality and oppression, while 54% interpreted the "God of Justice" on a personal level such as being fair in personal dealings. Clearly this demonstrates that **we must educate the parishioners more completely on the social teachings of the Catholic Church so that they understand the justice/advocacy component of our ministry as coming from our religious tradition.** *(St. Thomas Aquinas Catholic Church)*

Summary

One measure of your leadership is your sensitivity to the views of members throughout the congregation—but leadership is more than reading the opinion polls. The survey offers you an instrument for listening to a wider selection of voices focused on particular questions and responding at the same time. The results map the terrain, but they do not tell you the route to be taken. After listening, leaders must make decisions based on their own convictions about what God expects of us in particular situations.

We have noted briefly the kinds of information a survey might offer in response to questions of the church in its context and the members' views of congregational unity, confidence in decision making, faith in social ministry, time for volunteering, and understanding of social advocacy. You may wish to ask other questions that push the church or challenge its unity. Membership surveys, when planned and used sparingly, can inform church leaders and members, show a profile of large and small groups within the congregation, and lay the groundwork for self-understanding and stronger social ministry.

PART III

Organizing for Social Minis

All churches rely on the same foundations in mobilizing for social ministry. Congregations that know their turf have a clarity of task that gives a focus to their ministry: they know what they want to do. Churches that know where social ministry fits in their Christian identity have access to renewable energy: they know why they want to do it. The prerequisites for organizing are community awareness and membership commitment.

But churches organize differently. With wide differences among congregations in heritage, polity, culture, resources, and leadership styles, a single pattern of organization would be impossible. In our common concern for social ministry, we use the same basic tools and seek similar results, yet the way we mobilize in each congregation is unique to the people involved and the problems they face.

Organizing puts ideas on wheels, translates faith into action, and enables our vision for ministry to become a tangible reality. If we think of social context as the air we breathe and identity as the soul or center of our being, then organization is the bone and muscle that makes things happen. Organizing:

— clarifies our purposes in the struggle to achieve them;
— shows the depth and duration of our commitment;
— demands fresh resources and generates new energy;
— challenges narrow ideas and expands our experience;
— shapes our perceptions even as we shape its program;
— breaks old stereotypes and builds new alliances; and
— helps us touch the lives of others and be touched in return.

For all these reasons, we should be more delighted when our organization succeeds than dismayed when it fails. Organizing is not only hard work—it transforms us in the process.

An organization is not a fixed structure but a dynamic relationship among a group of people who have agreed to work for a common goal through separate tasks. We can make an organizational chart by mapping out the tasks, the people, and their relationships to one another. But there are no right answers, no clear-cut guidelines to measure its correctness. We can measure the effectiveness of an organization only against the goals it has established (and revised as needed), conditioned by the problems it has faced in working toward those goals. For a collection of many resources, see *Organizing for Social Change* by Kim Bobo, et al. (Washington: Seven Locks Press, 1991).

The task of organizing is a puzzle to be solved, not a blueprint to be followed. In this chapter I will discuss and give examples of the ways different congregations have handled several significant elements that you will face as you begin to organize your social ministry. I have grouped these elements into three steps. As with earlier steps, these can be done in any order or you can work on them concurrently:

STEP ONE: Build an Organization. We mobilize for social ministry in order to carry out a purpose in a particular setting, and the purpose and setting must be yoked in the organization. As you build a ministry, you will confront four challenges:

> Management Style: Finding authority for social ministry;
> Group Expectations: Planning together, working separately;
> Project Partners: Developing allies in ministry; and
> Sharing Ministry: Including consumers in basic decisions.

STEP TWO: Develop Resources to Support Your Ministry. Ministry requires many resources, but these three can make or break your program:

> Volunteers: Finding and keeping the right people;
> Fund Raising: Conquering your reluctance; and
> Project Staff: Shaping your most important decision.

STEP THREE: Clarify the Purpose of Your Ministry. In addition to organizing, your committee must interpret your ministry to other people. Often the greatest misunderstanding is between ministries that respond to the needs of individuals, and those that challenge ineffective and destructive institutions:

> Service Ministries: Acting with Christian compassion; and
> Justice Ministries: Challenging dysfunctional systems.

Build an Organization

Of the many aspects that contribute to good management, we find four most difficult: (a) How will you fit the social ministry into the existing congregational management style? (b) How will you hold a common vision, yet accomplish each step along the way? (c) How will you expand your base without losing your constituency? (d) How will your ministry empower the people you are trying to serve?

Management Style:
Finding Authority for Social Ministry

Guidelines

Here is the organizational dilemma: Your authority for social ministry is based on a combination of compassion for people in need (and anger about systems that need changing) and the resources available in your particular situation. Your study of the social context should have demonstrated a need for your ministry that you can state with force and clarity. But the shape and dynamics of the organization are always a compromise between the urgent community needs and all the baggage of congregational memories and community experiences. These memories and experiences are usually ambiguous, unstated, and sometimes even conflicting.

Overtly, the organization grows from the statement of need. As an organizer, however, you recognize that the opening statement of ministry is only half of the organizational rationale. The rest involves negotiating among individual and community values until you find the form of management that feels right to the people involved. We sometimes hear that "form follows function"—but forces far stronger shape these ministries.

Examples from Churches

A cooperative parish of three mainline congregations in a congested urban area developed the following management design. Notice how they begin with their focus for ministry and then show how the management is integral to the work to be done. Note the interlocking frameworks of authority, with no real barriers between church and agency authority, because the task is compelling. Imagine how different the organizational structure might have been if the sponsoring churches were more hierarchical or had a theology that demanded more direct congregational control:

> *Fountain Square C&C Project will **rehabilitate boarded-up houses in the neighborhood using volunteer labor to assist home ownership for low -income families** . . . These families will work with other volunteers in the rehab process, . . . earning credits toward a down payment in exchange for hours of work.*
>
> ***Management** of the ongoing project will be at three levels. **Policy decisions will be made by the Board of Governors** . . . The **working committees** of the board will be: executive, finances, personnel, operations, network relations, and advocacy. **The next level of management is through the auspices of the [community] Investment Corporation** . . . [that] has agreed to work with this project. **The third level of management is on-the-job.** There the person in charge will be the **construction engineer**, laying out the work, supervising the volunteer workers, coordinating the use of tools, and ordering supplies, etc. This person will have a working relationship with Investment Corporation, conferring with the architect assigned to the particular job, while answering to the personnel committee of the Board of Governors of the Church and Community Project.*
>
> *At the same level as the construction engineer and answering to the same personnel committee will be the **volunteer coordinator**.*

*This person will be a Church and Community worker. Viewed as
part of the pastoral team of the Fountain Square UMC assigned to
the work of the Church and Community Project, this person will
interrelate with life questions of volunteers and prospective
homeowners. (Edwin Ray United Methodist Church)*

In a more informal setting, this careful distribution of authority
might be inappropriate. Notice how this rural project with two cooperating churches begins with the program and lets the organization evolve
over time. Again, they open with a statement of purpose, but they pro-
ceed with a variety of community activities and allow the structure to
bubble up from that base:

*Since there has been no sense of community for many years, . . . the
residents of the community are seen as powerless to do anything
beyond individual households or land holdings to affect, nurture,
change or improve community life... Our first step is to develop a
sense of common purpose and discover our neighbors through a
series of organized activities.*

  *A sign-board will identify our community, and will tell about
planned community activities . . . The Core Committee will initially
be in charge of where it will be placed and what it will say. Later
the community board may expand, improve, control, etc. the sign-
board . . . Out of community meetings, committees will be established to develop facilities, finances and personnel. We envision the
first step as a small place with several tables and chairs that serves
drinks, donuts, and sandwiches at breakfast and lunch. (Deer Creek
Presbyterian Church)*

This Catholic parish reflects a radically different style of management. Although the leaders welcome input from a variety of sources,
they have no question about lines of authority. Working in this setting,
you would soon discover that the project staff report to the pastor, who,
along with the parish council, bears the responsibility for all significant
decisions:

*The ministry functions will be under the direction of a full-time
Director, to be hired by the Neighborhood Youth Committee. The*

*Director will serve on the St. Joan of Arc staff and will **report as
designated by the pastor in day-to-day operations**. The Youth
Committee will induct into its membership two neighborhood
youth—one a parishioner and one a non-Catholic neighbor. Matters of Policy will be decided upon by the Community Youth Committee and, if required, **approved by the Parish Council**. (St. Joan
of Arc Catholic Church)*

Delightfully, we cannot predict by polity the management patterns
that will be used by congregations in social ministry. We find independent ministries launched from Catholic churches and Protestant ministries that report directly to the pastor. You simply "gotta know the
territory," as, for example, with this Baptist congregation:

*The Steering Committee will agree upon and make **recommendations to the church** to be voted on during its business meeting once
a month. This committee will . . . recommend a Director for hire to
the church. **The church will have final authority in matters of
policy** . . . The Director will be accountable to the Steering Committee, with day-to-day **supervision by the Pastor**. (Cornell Baptist
Church)*

Although we have a bias for broad participation in decision making,
you are unlikely to break historic congregational patterns of authority by
direct confrontation. Rather, make the most of the leadership patterns
you find, at least in the initial stages of program development. Leadership styles should be measured by the ways they contribute to achieving
your ministry goals. Often leadership becomes more broadly participa-
tory as the ministry matures, especially as volunteers influence the
organization through the practice of ministry.

Group Expectations:
Planning Together, Working Separately

Guidelines

Organization allows your committee to share a common vision but to
divide the tasks so that various subgroups can work separately. In
organizing for ministry, some groups excel in the vision but never get
around to the tasks, while others generate so many tasks that they lose
the vision.

You can help resolve this dilemma by stating directly and simply
your dream for ministry and the steps it will take to reach your goals.
The more clearly you articulate the dream, the easier it is to define the
particular tasks that need to be done and agree on who will do them.

Examples from Churches

This Catholic-Protestant team, crossing cultural and denominational
differences, works hard to affirm their strong common bond while
defining distinct responsibilities:

> *St. Mary's Catholic Church and the First Congregational UCC of
> Canton, Il (known hereafter as the partnering churches) have
> chosen to call their project Christian Service Program . . . **Pastors**
> of the partnering churches, or their designated representatives, will
> be members of the Advisory Council. **Other Advisory members** . . .
> would include persons with specialized knowledge in areas such as:
> legal, fund-raising, grant-writing, public relations, and human
> resources. **Standing committees** will be formed for Fund-Raising,
> Building Management, Publicity, Program Administration, Advo-
> cacy and Human Resources. **Special committees** will be appointed
> as needed . . . **Each member church and its congregation are
> expected to provide** leadership, manpower, and financial support on
> specific needs and for annual operating expenses. (St. Mary's
> Catholic Church, Canton)*

In organizing to share the tasks, you need more help from realists
than from romantics. The lofty dream of this church—to begin a transi-

tional shelter for homeless families—came together because the committee was tough enough to plan together in the face of all that needed to get done. They followed a two-step approach to planning. First they surveyed all sorts of work to be done:

> *During the implementation year, the core committee in consultation with the partnering groups will put in place the particulars for the project including: securing and readying a facility; writing by-laws, operating procedures, job descriptions, and training manuals; developing programming and a general **record-keeping system;** recruiting, orienting, and **training staff** both paid and volunteer; **broadening our base** of partnering groups in the community; engaging in **fundraising** by asking individuals and groups for money and submitting grants to appropriate funding sources as well as developing a suitable financial record keeping system; and overseeing a study of the area homeless and the availability of low-cost housing of Lafayette County.*

Next they created subcommittees like this one, which refined the general plan to define what they needed to work on and what was beyond their scope:

> **Our plan** *is to acquire an economically efficient facility that can accommodate both individuals and families in a safe and secure environment until these persons can find normal living arrangements . . . As we currently envision this project, the **services** of the Transitional Housing Center would include meals, transportation, housing search and placement, and recreational activities. **Referrals** will be made for: financial assistance, child care, substance abuse, physical or emotional abuse, pastoral or long-term counseling, job readiness and literacy skills, job training, budget and money management counseling, housekeeping skills, parenting skills, hygiene and nutrition education, and health assessment screening including necessary health care. (St. Boniface Catholic Church)*

Your ministry will be different from this one, but clear statements of expectations will be no less important. Sometimes when you know what must be done you can capture both the common vision and the essential tasks in a few well-chosen words:

*During the first year, we will address the critical issues that must be resolved before an **adult day care facility** can be established in our neighborhood: **money, location and management**. (University Park Christian Church)*

By stating clearly your group expectations, you can see the direction to move and the tasks to be done. You have not reduced your work, but you have named it and established the place to begin.

Project Partners: Developing Allies in Ministry

Guidelines

Because no congregation has the physical, spiritual, and financial resources to make a significant impact alone, many reach out to neighboring churches and concerned social agencies to join them in ministry. Some partners join as peers, carrying equally the joys and burdens of developing social ministry. Others may come as allies in a coalition, each with a special contribution to offer, yet with more limited authority and liability. Whatever their role, you are looking for partners who will strengthen and extend your ministry. The challenge of partnership is to expand your vision with new resources, without reducing your congregation's sense of ownership and commitment to the ministry program.

Examples from Churches

In this program, several community churches came together to form a senior citizens' center. They are clear about their hopes for expanded resources through shared authority:

*The partners will be an **integral part of the Center** organizational structure . . . Seats given to the Partners on the Board of Directors will insure continuity and ongoing involvement. Each Partner must secure the full cooperative backing from their organization in writing. A Financial **commitment** will be sought from the Partners in whatever form their organizational structure permits, i.e. **financial grant, fund raising, membership, donated equipment, public-***

*ity, etc. Partners will hold full Executive Board and Committee Officer and Committee positions. **Volunteer staff** from the Partners will be recruited, trained, and utilized. (Irvington United Methodist Church)*

In rural towns where social, financial, political, and religious organizations draw from a much smaller pool of leaders, we often find that an apparently wide variety of partners are often the same people wearing different hats. In following rural partnership, the number of people involved was fewer than the number of organizations listed:

*To date we have commitments for support and volunteers from the Burnettsville Town Board, Burnettsville Community Board, Washington Township Trustee, Burnettsville State Bank, Burnettsville Senior Citizens Club, and the Burnettsville Mennonite Fellowship. **We expect to work closely** with them in operation and fund-raising. (First Baptist Church)*

Partners come at a price. They complicate decision making, even as they broaden horizons and resources. You may recognize the feelings behind this experience:

*We assume that the four groups with **differing traditions and motivations, yet similar visions,** will be able to amicably address policy decisions and arrive at consensus. We are still struggling with how much control/authority Hope Church should rightfully expect to exercise. (Hope Presbyterian Church)*

Beyond incorporating institutional partners, you can expand the community base of your ministry by creating a structure for individual memberships. This kind of grass-roots participation helps in virtually any kind of social ministry, from youth groups to elderly respite and from child care to peace lobbies:

*A membership-based organization is one that gets its **power and direction through the grassroots**. It has the most potential for empowering members and those involved, through education, experience, organizing, and advocacy. We do not want to start a*

*senior citizen center that only provides services and does not
empower seniors or community members . . . We proposed that the
Lacon Community Center be a membership based organization,
meaning that the **members will direct the organization through a
board of directors**. (Immaculate Conception Catholic Church)*

Partnerships and memberships broaden the base, increase the impact, and transform the leadership of the ministry—when you expand without losing the commitment of your congregation.

Sharing Ministry: Including Consumers in Basic Decisions

Guidelines

We minister **with** people, not **for** them. When we do ministry for people, we reduce them to objects. "They" and "we" are different. "They" are called the "clients," the "program consumers," or the "target population." With our resources we are powerful, and with their needs they are weak. As the providers of ministry, we are the decision makers, and they are the recipients.

Sharing ministry **with people** requires more effort. We noted above that partnerships are difficult among groups with different leadership styles, educational backgrounds, and available resources. Sharing ministry with the consumers we want to reach also crosses such social barriers as power, socio-economic status, culture, age, and lifestyle. Bridging these differences inevitably complicates the ministry.

We make the effort to share ministry across these boundaries because we believe that all people are equal in the forgiving love of God. The purpose of our ministry is to share the empowering grace of God, not to invent new forms of dependency. Once we have experienced shared ministry, we recognize the inadequacy of more hierarchical models.

With each new generation of program participants comes the challenge to find appropriate ways for sharing ministry between those who begin by giving and others who begin by receiving.

Examples from Churches

At the minimum, your ministry should listen to and learn from the experiences of people who have been through your program. You can
incorporate this kind of simple evaluation into almost any social ministry:

> *Ongoing **evaluation** will be an important role of the committee to
> gain feedback from the clientele being served and making recom-
> mendations for changes in policy or expansion of services.
> (Westminster Presbyterian Church)*

The only real experts on the needs and emotions of the people you
are trying to reach are the people themselves. No matter how well your
volunteers understand the conditions, empathy is not the same as having
lived the problems. Some groups have drawn volunteers and trainers of
volunteers from the ranks of those who have found the program helpful.
Other ministries find that consumer perspectives are essential to the
decision making of the board. Housing ministries, for example, have
incorporated their new residents on their policy boards, and some kinds
of programs for the elderly are virtually administered by the participants.

If you are concerned that the voices of one or two consumers might
be stifled on a larger board, you might consider creating a separate
structure to hear their views and develop their independent leadership
skills:

> *In an effort to encourage neighborhood youth participation in policy
> decisions, **a Youth Council**, composed of persons being served by
> the project [helps] the Director and the Committee benefit from the
> **thoughts and feelings of the participants**. (St. Joan of Arc Catholic
> Church)*

In whatever way it works best for you, your ministry will be stronger if you empower the recipients and affirm the equality of all participants in building a better community, under God. The process of ministry is an important part of its product.

Summary

When you have recognized your leadership style, defined the tasks you need to do, found allies with a common sense of ministry, and invited consumers to share in shaping your program, then organization is simply your modus operandi. The best organization is the way you get things done, because it accomplishes the goals of your ministry.

Develop Resources to Support Your Ministry

You will need many resources for launching your social ministry, including a broad base of support, continuous interpretation, space to house your program, equipment, and materials. These needs vary widely among different kinds of programs. One advocacy program for the hearing impaired had very modest space needs: "an office . . . access to a copy machine . . . storage for brochures, envelopes, and supplies . . . and work space for volunteers" (Ridge Lutheran Church). A youth program, on the other hand, needed "an arena where the teens can play their music" (West Park Christian Church). Someone suggested that these projects should be combined since only the hearing impaired could comfortably share space with the teens' music.

But some kinds of needs are universal. These three seem the most challenging in all types of social ministry: (a) How will you find your essential volunteers? (b) How will you fund your ministry? (c) How will you decide about paid staff?

Volunteers: Finding and Keeping the Right People

Guidelines

Volunteers are the essence of church-based ministries in which members express their faith in action. They are not simply a grudging concession to the absence of money to pay staff. Volunteer ministries continue because members find their personal faith and church loyalty strengthened in exercising love, touching the lives of others and being touched in return. In empowering others, we ourselves become more alive.

Your volunteers can do what professional agencies cannot do or would not attempt. Often churches offer the only commuynity space in a residential area and the only trusted place in an unsafe neighborhood. Churches can break through the isolation of elderly people who live scattered around the community, aggressively seek teen-agers who have been abandoned by other agencies, or begin night ministries where the police are the only alternative. Churches can provide a personal touch in the tutoring of children or mediate reconciliation between victims and offenders.

With dogged commitment and ingenious creativity, by faith your volunteers can do what social agencies cannot. But they do it as volunteers, and so they have different incentives and satisfactions, different leadership and management needs, and different standards of success. Your volunteers are generally not professional social workers, but just people who care about people. Volunteers are as much the recipients of the program as are the clients with whom they work. Your volunteers are your primary resource, the foundation of a church-based social ministry. For additional help, see *How to Mobilize Church Volunteers* by Marlene Wilson (Minneapolis: Augsburg, 1983).

It takes planning and imagination to make the best use of volunteers. The challenge is to link their faith motivation with your organizational program in ways that satisfy both.

Examples from Churches

In defining the tasks your committee faces, the cultivation and support of your volunteers is as important as your program and administration. One group defines the whole job with disarming simplicity:

The work is 1/3 program hours, 1/3 preparation, and 1/3 organization of volunteers. (Cornell Baptist Church)

Volunteers bring a diversity of gifts that could not be found in any one staff professional. Typically, volunteers are interested in three broad areas: the hands-on work of ministry, support of the organization, and advocacy for changes in social structures that affect people's lives. This committee plans for all three types of involvement:

Every effort will be made to involve people in the work of the Lacon Center. The Senior Citizen Survey indicates there may be room for **volunteering in the areas of hospitality, transportation, yard work, light maintenance,** *and others. Volunteers will be involved in* **organizational matters** *as board members, keeping records and writing the newsletter. Most of the* **advocacy work, including letter writing and programs,** *will be handled by volunteers. (Immaculate Conception Catholic Church)*

Since every situation is different, you will need to find your own ways to involve the maximum number of interested people. Even when members are unavailable at the time a program operates, you may be able to involve them in program support and interpretation:

We cannot supply many volunteers because most of our members work during the day. However, we will sponsor **fund-raising din-ners.** *We will host volunteers when they come for* **orientation** *to the program and the neighborhood. We will* **publicize** *the program by going door-to-door in the neighborhood, and will* **sponsor the open house** *at the beginning of the school year. (Avondale Presbyterian Church)*

Volunteers fear most not knowing what is expected of them. Some volunteers want to know precisely the duties they are to perform, and others want the challenge of solving problems for which no clear guide-lines exist. In either case, someone must take the responsibility for incorporating volunteers, training them, and demonstrating our apprecia-tion:

Another facet of the program . . . is **Volunteer Development and Training.** *The development of a volunteer cadre will be the prime responsibility of the youth committee, but training of volunteers will be done by the Project Director. (St. Joan of Arc Catholic Church)*

You can measure the success of your volunteer program because volunteers vote with their feet. The number of volunteers you can involve in every possible way is the best index of program support throughout the congregation, and they are the most convincing interpret-ers of the ministry to the church and the larger community:

*By maintaining a constant flow of information between project
leaders and the congregation, we hope that members become
individually excited about the mission of the project; that they will
express personal concern about the issues the project addresses
and **share this concern** with one another; that individual members
become **more committed to the church** as an agent to address
change, and become **more willing to serve.** (Hope Presbyterian
Church)*

For all their enthusiasm in other areas, program volunteers rarely
raise money unless they are specifically asked. It is important that you
begin by recognizing that and working with your volunteers within their
perspectives. But in time you will also want to help them see how
important they are in the larger framework of the ministry and how they
can help support the program in a variety of ways—sometimes financially.

Fund Raising: Conquering Your Reluctance

Guidelines

Money problems are emotional barriers to the development of many
social ministries. Churches have budgeted for their own needs, including
established benevolences. They have a pattern of giving that they understand and anticipate continuing, and they may find it hard to imagine
supporting a new social ministry within their current financial situation.
After years of effort, they feel that the church income is fixed—or worse,
it is declining. They often cannot see the needs for community ministry
simply because they cannot imagine that they have the resources to make
any difference.

The challenge of fund raising is to find new sources of revenue to
support the social ministry without undermining the current budget for
all the other commitments of the congregation. The first step is an
expanded concept of stewardship.

In many congregations stewardship is the name for the specific fund
raising program that supports the worship, educational, and fellowship
life of the church. But if we expand stewardship to embrace the use of

all God's gifts to support and strengthen all God's people, then we have access to a much larger array of community resources.

When you see your social ministry as God's instrument to touch individuals and transform the community, then your committee can approach businesses and individuals outside the church membership. Because the church cares about the community, you can ask corporations, foundations, and even agencies of government to join in your outreach. If your sense of stewardship includes caring for the community through and beyond the church membership, you can open a whole range of new financial resources not otherwise available to self-contained congregational programs. For many practical suggestions see *The Grass Roots Fundraising Book* by Joan Flanagan (Chicago: Contemporary Books, 1982).

Volunteer ministries generally do not need massive financial support; the support required depends on your goals and your plans to achieve them. Personnel is the most significant cost variable, and volunteer programs reduce staff costs. Tutoring and other youth programs tend to have minimal budgets, while pantries and meal programs generally need some staff. Counseling and day-care programs often require professionals, and housing programs usually demand substantial financing. But when matched with comparable professional agencies, churches are able to provide more services at lower cost through the use of volunteers, low overhead, and in-kind contributions.

While you will not need the large budget of a professional agency, you will need a midrange of funding. In most cases the money can be found "through prayer and fasting"—which might be translated "through imagination and hard work."

Examples from Churches

Financial support is so significant that you should confront the problem directly with a committee that makes fund raising their primary task:

> *A volunteer chairperson and subcommittee from the churches and the community . . . have no other task for the project but to seek out funds. (First-Meridian Heights Presbyterian Church)*

Since ninety percent of charitable giving comes from individuals,

you should aggressively tell your story to particular people throughout
your community. Smaller towns may have fewer resources, but the
people who live there have more access to each other, as seen in the
planning of this small town housing project to attract the attention of
their neighbors:

> *We will continue to request **donations from individuals** within our
> community. We will let them know about the tax credits to individu-
> als and businesses who invest in development that provides low and
> moderate income housing . . . [We will] have a **work-a-thon** where
> volunteers work on a project (elderly persons' home needing a new
> roof). The volunteers get other people to sponsor them . . . We will
> paint a **giant thermometer** and put it in a prominent place in town
> with our goal at the top. As we advertise our needs and educate the
> community, we will let all know where we stand in donations . . . We
> will develop a **mailing list of donors**. They will be kept informed
> about how our project is proceeding, when unexpected needs arise,
> and successes by mail. We will **express thanks** as we meet our
> goals. (Washburn Christian Church)*

Your denominational body may have sources of funding that you
should explore, both through the formal agencies of the church and in the
informal networks among pastors or churches:

> *Funding will come from **grants, from suburban churches, Metro
> Ministries, District, Conference, and National Division Mission
> sources of the United Methodist Church**. (Edwin Ray United
> Methodist Church)*

Small town neighbors and denominational ties reflect the importance of personal connections in fund raising: people give to other
people they know and trust, in small towns and big cities alike.

Although sometimes local and well-known sources are sufficient,
you may need a more diversified approach to support your ministry.
Notice how this committee begins with the sources that are nearest and
most involved in the ministry, and then moves out to seek funding from
other agencies that share their concern. Although they are church-based,
they recognize possible sources that churches often ignore:

Initially, we expect the fund-raising program to cover the following sources: 1) The **contract and partnering organizations** *will be contacted to determine the amount of financial support available from each. 2) A prospective donor list will be developed of* **individuals in the community** *who might be able and willing to contribute financially to the project. 3) A listing will be developed of all* **corporations** *which have some relationship to the community or the project and contact will be made to determine the proper approach to request corporate financial support. 4) From resource listing of* **foundations,** *contact will be made to determine procedures for developing the opportunities for financial support and preparation of grant proposals. 5) Public sector* **government agencies** *will be contacted to determine any programs which might provide financial support for the project. 6) When appropriate,* **user fees based on a sliding scale** *will be established. (Irvington United Methodist Church)*

As a source of energy, money never replaces Christian commitment, but without financial resources the best intentions cannot be sustained. One ministry approaches fund raising like the biblical injunctions for prayer: "Seek and you shall find; knock and it will be opened to you" (Matthew 7:7).

Project Staff: Shaping Your Most Important Decision

Guidelines

As your ministry increases in scope and complexity, you will probably consider employing staff. Choosing one person, or part-time work from one or more people, can resolve nagging organizational problems and make a significant difference in stabilizing a church-based social ministry.

But this is also the most unpredictable element in building a ministry program. Selecting and supervising staff is an Achilles' heel even for well-organized, fully supported programs.

It can be awkward to bring a paid staff person into a program operated and served by volunteers. Although job definitions, expectations, and accountabilities may be clearly stated, the lines between volunteers and paid staff are never sufficiently precise to cover every circumstance. Consider the dilemma if some volunteers relax their efforts because the staff is "paid to do the job," while others feel offended that the same staff person has "taken over." Under pressure, volunteers and staff can become suspicious of each other's motives.

Further, in a new church-based ministry the staff is often less experienced and underpaid, compared with employees of more established, professional agencies; yet the volunteers work for nothing. Compensation may be a continuing problem. The board leaders, even the pastor, may be equally inexperienced in supervising staff. In addition, social ministries that are responsive to community needs are often growing and changing. Particularly in newly organized ministries, initial job descriptions rapidly become outdated and need to be changed. Both volunteers and staff need to amend their ways of thinking and interpret agreements flexibly—sometimes an invitation to conflict.

You will need a sustaining faith, a trust in people, and a strong dose of good humor to incorporate staff into your voluntary program.

Examples from Churches

You may wish to begin with part-time staff. Notice the qualifications for these part-time employees. They are expected to have values similar to the volunteers, but knowledge and cultural affinity that go beyond the skills and sensitivities of the current church members:

> *We feel that in order to run a strong program we will need to **hire three people on a part-time basis**: a director who will be in charge of planning the program and running it, and two assistants. We do not feel that these paid staff must have specific academic qualifications. We are looking for men and women who **love children** and enjoy working with them. We would prefer people from the general area, people who **know city life** and the dynamics of Chicago neighborhoods. Because of the high number of Hispanics in the neighborhood, we plan to hire one **bilingual worker** so communication with Hispanic parents can be facilitated. (Avondale Presbyterian Church)*

Whatever the qualifications, you will need to be especially clear about the responsibilities and accountability of staff, while not being so detailed that the job description inhibits personal initiative or prohibits growth with the maturing of the ministry:

> _A paid **Director will direct and manage** the project, plan the day-to-day program, organize and manage volunteers, supervise other paid staff, record attendance/effectiveness measures, and be responsible for publicity. The Director will be a member of the Advisory Board and an ex-officio, non-voting member of the steering committee. As such, the Director may make suggestions to the Steering Committee on matters of policy. The Director will be **accountable to the Steering Committee with day-to-day supervision by the pastor.** (Cornell Baptist Church)_

Some committees expect growth and transition. Although change may not occur in the anticipated way, such language invites similar flexibility in other aspects of the program:

> _The positions of construction engineer and volunteer coordinator will be needed long range. The bookkeeper-financial officer is **expected to go from being an unpaid volunteer to one with a stipend** through a retired volunteers program. (Edwin Ray United Methodist Church)_

For the protection of both the board and the employee, include a procedure for employee review, affirmation, evaluation, and new directions:

> _[The employee] will have an opportunity **quarterly for formal interchange regarding job satisfaction and performance.** Disagreements will be brought to the attention of the **board of managers for a final resolution.** (First-Meridian Heights Presbyterian Church)_

The right staff person often gives credit for transforming the program by bringing new levels of satisfaction to everyone who participates. You should approach the choice recognizing that this is probably the single most important decision your board will make.

Clarify the Purpose of Your Ministry

As a planning group, you are responsible for interpreting your ministry to other people. Interpretation depends upon clear project goals and effective communication. Yet even in the throes of organizing, many committees remain divided on the goals of their efforts. The most pervasive difference is between an emphasis on helping individuals and a focus on changing social systems. Different assumptions about the causes and solutions of social problems support these two perspectives; their proponents see the same world quite differently.

Christians who emphasize individual responsibility for human behavior see the purpose of social ministries as caring for particular people who need help. For biblical warrants they may point to Jesus' ministry, from his first announcement in Nazareth (Luke 4:18-19) to the Son of Man judging the nations on the quality of care for "the least of these who are members of my family" (Matthew 25:31-46).

Other Christians would shift the burden of social problems away from individual responsibility, placing it at least equally on the ways in which various social, political, economic, and religious institutions have limited and frustrated "the poor and the oppressed." For biblical precedent they often reach back to the prophetic traditions and forward into early church literature in James and Revelation.

Sharp disagreements between commitments to service and to justice have put many social ministry programs on the rocks of irreconcilable differences. Yet other groups embrace these two views as ancient and honorable perspectives—two sides of the same coin, each with an imprint of its own and both necessary in the fullness of ministry.

As the group most directly responsible for the development of your ministry, your committee is a primary source for interpreting the purpose and meaning of the program. You can exacerbate these differences, or you can find a yoke to harness them together for the sake of a stronger program and for people from the larger community who would like to support your ministry—sometimes for different reasons.

Service Ministries: Acting with Christian Compassion

Guidelines

Ministries of service to individuals may seem most natural to your church planning committee. These caring activities reflect the personal quality of relationships among the members of most congregations. Even large churches see themselves as caring communities, especially when individuals are infirm or troubled. Both our faith and our culture highly value this personal, individual care.

Reflecting this emphasis on each individual, your church may approach social ministry as a natural expression of faith in response to human need. In describing your ministry this way, you can mobilize some of the strongest Christian values prized by your church members. In narrative and in pictures, most church literature interpreting social ministry depicts the compassion of our ministries in response to the needs of particular persons—the vulnerable child, the broken family, the isolated elderly adult.

Caring runs a risk, however, of perpetuating inequality. Your committee may need to push the congregation to understand social ministry as something more than providing help for less fortunate people. Reflecting faith communities that witness to God's transforming power, church social ministries should encourage and empower individuals to grow into the fullness of their God-given possibilities. Ministries to individual needs may at one time be as supportive as a mother's love, yet may later become as inhibiting as a parent who hangs onto children long after they are grown.

Your committee can shape a ministry of service that will care for people when they need help and will also empower people to faith and personal fulfillment. You can help members of the congregation to grow by including them in events that help both "server and servee" to mature together. For those without direct contact with your program, you can

have an impact by the way you help them understand what their church
is doing in ministry.

Examples from Churches

Youth are a primary concern for many social ministries, for they represent the next generation, the future of the church and the community:

> *As our project begins, we will target the young people of our*
> *neighborhood. **We will address their needs** in the particulars of*
> *Education and Life-Skills; Health, Recreation and Faith Develop-*
> *ment; Employment and Economic Betterment. Our program will*
> *consist of Formal Tutoring, Counseling, Advocacy Referrals and*
> *Organized Sports. (St. Joan of Arc Catholic Church)*

Notice how this ministry begins with a focus on the needs of the
elderly but moves toward strengthening whole families:

> *Daybreak Inc. will provide an **adult day health care service** for the*
> *community. The project will offer older adults the opportunity to*
> *maintain or improve their level of functioning enabling them to*
> *remain in a private home setting for as long as possible . . . In*
> *addition, the project will **improve the relationships among family***
> ***members** coping with the stress of care-giving. (Community United*
> *Church of Christ)*

Some programs combine the needs of one group with the skills of
another. In this project the teenagers learn home repair and maintenance
while the elderly have their homes repaired. The combined effect will
change the community attitude and climate:

> *We want to work together to **train people who are unskilled**, in-*
> *cluding High School students, to learn maintenance and repair*
> *through **restoring property in need of improvement** in our commu-*
> *nities. We will be doing one property at a time, when needed, as*
> *supervising personnel is available. Our goal is to **strengthen***
> ***community pride and renew hope** for the future. (Washburn*
> *Christian Church)*

Empowerment is the primary focus of the next ministry, which addressed the captivity of poor families and challenged church members to break the cycle as partners with the poor. Although their empowerment language reflects the influence of liberation theology, their focus is clearly on individuals and families, not on changing the systems in which these people live:

> *Empowering people to help themselves and their community will be our goal in Family Partners. Inviting poverty level persons with a desire to **exit the cycle of dependency** to partner with others who care will be the direction for the project. Through a process of shared decision making and goal setting, the project intends to assist partner families to realize **internal personal resources** and **external community resources**. (Baptist Temple)*

You can ground your service ministry in congregational and community commitments to respond to people who need help. If helping the needy is your only motive, however, you may create new dependencies. By seeking ways of empowering others, you strengthen both those who are served and those who provide the service.

Justice Ministries:
Challenging Dysfunctional Systems

Guidelines

Ministries of justice begin with a different assumption. Although they may be equally concerned with individual growth, they place a far greater emphasis on the havoc caused by ineffective and destructive systems. They insist that the primary burden for our social problems rests with such dysfunctional systems as the educational institutions that leave students illiterate, employment programs that ignore the displaced worker, government housing agencies that cannot shelter those who need it most, police who break the law more than enforce it, and courts that neither satisfy the victims nor reclaim the criminals.

Justice ministries point the finger of responsibility toward the institutions that not only fail in their tasks but leave people scared and unable to find a foothold in society. They want to confront the sources of the problems rather than blame the victims of these failing institutions.

This emphasis on justice seems foreign to church members whose primary focus is on serving people in need. Justice ministries challenge inadequate systems, while service ministries help needy people. Justice ministries use collective, confrontational tactics to change institutions, while service ministries use personal relationships to strengthen individuals and families. Justice advocates changes in policies and programs, while service seeks support for individuals in transition. And the two often misunderstand each other: justice sees service as avoiding the basic issues, while service views justice as stirring up the waters, making the problems worse.

The challenge you face as leaders is to find bridges that can affirm both styles of social ministry. Their foundations are different, but their goals can be combined.

Examples from Churches

The sharp distinctions that seem so theologically clear quickly blur in the practice of ministry. Notice how easily this youth program slides from advocacy for the needs of individual students to advocacy for changes in the educational system:

> *TLM's commitment to social justice expresses itself through **advocacy with parents, teachers, employers, and legislators.** The TLM director will stay in direct communication with both parents and employers as a teen advocate, and . . . the local High School to determine the progress of TLM's teenagers and to intervene as necessary. This may lead to intervention with the school Board on policy matters or other intervention at the local level. (Good News Community Church)*

The leaders of this elderly care program are much more aware of the distinction between service and justice and of a progression from one to the other. They build on a network of service agencies and the trust of clients as a foundation for pressing for legislative changes regarding Alzheimer's disease:

*Advocacy is defined as pleading another person's cause and is also
understood as "treating the disease not the symptoms." One of the
goals of adult day care is to provide services to both the participants and care giver families, facilitating **integration into the community's health and social network.** As we gain experience and
trust of clients and care givers we will be constantly alert for other
areas where we may become effective advocates. A case in point
may be raising public consciousness on the **need for legislation** to
identify Alzheimer's and related disorders as a health condition
qualifying for Medicare and insurance coverage. (Community
United Church of Christ)*

This group in a rural town has been hit by a recession of the farm
economy and a cutback in regional industrial employment. They are
seeking ways to deal with their triple problems of declining income, lost
employment, and deteriorating housing. But, like most effective justice
ministries, they do not seek to act alone. Rather, they have formed a
council or coalition to translate the relational issues of service ministries
into challenges for systemic change:

*We will continue to study the root cause of poverty, unemployment,
and poor housing. We feel we must take social action plus service
to minister properly to the poor . . . [We have] **a community council
with a legislative agenda** for support of the jobless including legislation concerning plant closings and layoffs, and mortgage foreclo-
sures. (Washburn Christian Church)*

An urban housing ministry understands its work as far more than
construction and renovation. The community has not been transformed
until the residents have a say in the policies that shape the future of the
area. In this situation the project leaders recognize the oppression of
intangible economic and political forces, but they lift up the Christian
vision of a fully integrated neighborhood that looks beyond the necessities and welcomes the gifts each person brings. In their project goals
they have comfortably yoked housing for individual families with
transformation of the community:

One of the continuing responsibilities of the core committee is advocacy for [with] the poor . . . **To stand with them, to be present to their struggles, to interpret meaningfully** *the work of the* project *. . . are responsibilities of the core committee . . . It must work with constancy to hold up the* **vision** *of an economically (as well as in other ways)* **integrated neighborhood,** *which honors the right to the* **necessities of life** *for everyone, and which appreciates that* **all people have their gifts to offer to the community if their voices are heard and their confidence empowered.** *Linked with this is discerning what blocks the informant from available resources.*

Also, the core committee will be **supportive of these families as they organize** *to change city policies, patterns and decisions of banks and other institutions that function to seriously limit options which should rightfully be theirs if they are to function responsibly. (Edwin Ray United Methodist Church)*

Summary

Your project interpretation must clarify purpose and mobilize resources. The energy of your project will depend upon volunteers, fund raising, and staff. In organizing for your ministry, you will need to shape numerous elements to fit your identity, including managerial style, group expectations, partner development, and the empowerment of people with whom you are working. The whole task is dynamic: each part is interdependent, and no part is so completely finished that it no longer needs your attention. Organization just keeps on happening.

In building your organization, your goal is not a blueprint or a managerial chart. Rather, you should shape an organization that fits your situation, finds fresh energy in the congregation's faith, and, above all, is appropriate to get the job done.

Mobilizing Your Ministry

You can choke to death on too much material as easily as starve to death on too little. I wrote this book because in our work we have found too little material drawn from the actual experiences of churches in developing social ministries. Reviewing the collected sources of this book, I recognize that there is too much to digest at any one time. This is not a single story to be told in one sitting, but a variety of stories that need to be added to the conversation when necessary. I hope that the wide variety and earthy particularity will provide resources for congregational leaders to deal with the problems that are bound to occur in mobilizing for ministry.

Specifically, we find congregational committees for social ministry are most apt to get bogged down at predictable places. I will list a few of these common problem areas, not to suggest that you can avoid them altogether, but to offer solace and suggestions when you find yourselves in these quandaries as you move to develop or expand your ministry.

First, **leadership** is basic to developing your ministry. But finding the "one right leader" is rarely enough. Rather, as your ministry matures different people must step forward to take those responsibilities for which they seemed best suited. Strength lies more in the discovery and succession of leadership than in the strength of the initial group. A basic job of all leaders is to groom your replacements.

Second, **pastoral support** is crucial to the ministry, but the importance and the style of pastoral leadership vary greatly depending on cultural and denominational traditions and the particular people involved. Your social concern committee can do well, sometimes even better, without hands-on pastoral leadership, but not without the pastor's vocal, public support.

Third, **broad participation** is the backbone of strong ministry. Although we endorse the need for a small, committed core committee, both the knowledge and the work of ministry must be shared with a larger group far beyond the immediate leaders. We noted many examples of the importance of frequent project interpretation and a creative use of numerous volunteers. Bluntly said, in our experience the absence of broad participation and support is the single most frequent cause of project failure.

Fourth, since **planning** is a weakness of many efforts toward ministry, we encourage core groups to plan in a way that is appropriate to your task, leadership, and cultural context. Throughout our experience we see a wide variety of planning styles that work, but a nonplanning style never helps. Clarity of goals helps to keep the committee going in the face of interesting distractions and the inevitable moments of discouragement and despair. Planning specific steps helps members to know what each should be doing next. Whatever the particular style, successful planning generally has committed leaders, clear goals, and specific steps—and then makes the most of whatever happens.

Fifth, **theological pragmatism**—making the most of whatever happens—is both an attitude and a strategy. The attitude assumes that since God can use this and every moment, there must be something in this experience that is consistent with your goal. Pragmatism turns the attitude into action. Most social ministries achieve some of their basic goals, but most do it differently than they originally anticipated. The gift is knowing when to hang on to your initial vision and when to amend the particulars to achieve your larger goals.

Sixth, mobilize **congregational identity** in support of social ministry. Embedded in the energy of the memory of virtually every church are the biblical precedents, canonic and creedal statements, stories of events, and particular people that can be mobilized as forerunners and rationale for your ministries of compassion and justice. Some core committees assume a martyr-like loneliness that fails to use the strength of church history and may alienate your natural allies in the present composition of church members. Regardless of present practices, every congregation has a reservoir of memories and models on which to build programs of social ministry.

Seventh, claim the **gift of ministry**. As a burden laid on us for the sake of others or an organization that we must carry, social ministries can exhaust and burn out some very strong and loving people. But social ministry can be a gift that energizes staff, invigorates volunteers, and enlivens congregations in the act of reaching out to others. It happens when you recognize your resources and your limits and do not try to do it all alone. Sometimes you can find the additional help locally in pastors and others in the community. Sometimes specialists should be called in as resources to share their expertise, wider experience, and perspective. Sometimes you must simply back off–"let go and let God"—in a weekend retreat or other times of recognizing our human limitations. But ministry must remain a gift, and when that ceases perhaps it's time to begin again.

Beginning with the creative energy of our God, an awareness of some of the needs of your community, and the compassion and justice of our faith, you have all the resources necessary for social ministry in your community.

Brief Descriptions of Churches and Projects Included in this Book

Avondale Presbyterian Church, in a culturally diversified section of Chicago, developed TAP, The Afterschool Program, to combat a broad decline in interest and participation in local schools by educationally stimulating primary school children.

Community Covenant Church of Calumet Park, Illinois, is located in a middle-class Chicago suburb that recently experienced racial transition from white to African-American. They began an Educational Resource Center to offer GED classes and tutoring through a program of peer support for teens and young adults in the neighborhood.

Community United Church of Christ is one of the oldest congregations in the bedroom community of Morton, Illinois. Through Daybreak, Inc., this church and seven others offer care for the frail elderly, providing social enrichment and health care to participants and respite to caregiving families.

Cornell Baptist Church meets in a large renovated home in a racially mixed community near a major university in Chicago. The small congregation actively supports STRIVE as a Christian ministry of tutoring and enrichment activities for elementary school children, while working to empower parents to improve their school.

Deer Creek Presbyterian Church and manse stand alone in the fields with a scattering of houses across the highway and a mailing address of Camden, Indiana. With their nearest neighbor, **Faith Lutheran Church**, they generated Active Care Develops Community, which seeks to develop a sense of community through social events, physical improvements, and eventually a community center.

Douglas Park Covenant Church combines an older Swedish-heritage congregation with the younger **Iglesia del Pacto Evangelico de Douglas Park** (each under one hundred members) on the crowded West Side of Chicago. Together they created the Marshall Square-Douglas Park Family Education Center, which offers after-school tutoring, activities, and parenting education.

Edwin Ray United Methodist Church and two other small United Methodist congregations (each under 100 members) in the Fountain Square area of Indianapolis, Indiana, sponsor the Fountain Square Church and Community Project, which works for community renewal through better housing. In their low-income community, the project uses a large number of volunteers, including a teen-age skills training program to rehabilitate homes for purchase on a "sweat equity" basis and to provide home repair for older residents.

First Baptist Church of Burnettsville, Indiana (population 500), sponsors the Burnettsville Community Youth Center in the recently renovated gym of the old abandoned school building. They offer an after-school program for school-age children involving community volunteers of all ages.

First-Meridian Heights Presbyterian Church is a substantial congregation with 500 members and a significant endowment, located on the margin between racially and culturally different communities in Indianapolis, Indiana. Along with three neighboring congregations, they hired a community organizer and opened the Kaleidoscope Youth Center with programs in substance abuse prevention, nutrition, life skills, and mediation training for at-risk youth, particularly gang members.

First Presbyterian Church, Canton, is a congregation of about 400 in a Central Illinois town. Working with a neighboring Wesleyan Methodist church, they developed a resource exchange program through which town residents help meet each other's needs.

Fisher United Methodist Church, located in a small Illinois town, was strongly influenced by changing family patterns that left children unattended in the afternoons. In response the church began the Fisher Key Club, offering educational enrichment for "latchkey" children.

Good News Community Church/Iglesia Buenas Nuevas is a small congregation composed of Anglos, Latinos, and African-Americans in a low-income, racially mixed neighborhood of Chicago. It created the Teen Life Ministries program to provide safe space for youth and a variety of educational, social, and enrichment activities.

Hope Presbyterian Church has a small (200) but well-educated membership of professionals and managers in a suburb-like area of Springfield, Illinois. Faced with a need to expand their building, the church embraced Hope for the Nineties, a partnership of three community agencies with the church; together they serve infants, elderly, and families in crisis with active programs that utilize the new building all day every day.

Immaculate Conception Catholic Church (300) and three mainline Protestant congregations in the river town of Lacon, Illinois, constructed the Lacon Area Community Center. Through this facility they provide daily meals, socializing, and advocacy for elderly citizens and space for other groups including Head Start (the only such program in the county), a nursery school, teen dances, 4H, and other community groups.

Immanuel Lutheran Church, with a sanctuary that reflects its Swedish Lutheran immigrant heritage, sponsors Project New Start, a program of employment training and English classes for Indochinese immigrants. Although the sponsoring church is located in a middle-class Chicago residential community, their partner **Lutheran Chinese Christian Church** finds space in a mini-Chinatown of restaurants, shops, and professional services.

Irvington United Methodist Church is a large (1,000) but aging congregation with an English Tudor sanctuary in an economically diversified community of Indianapolis, Indiana. Its ecumenical ministry through the Irvington Senior Center offers a variety of services and social opportunities for isolated elderly throughout the community.

Lafayette Church of the Brethren maintains a strong heritage but attracts fewer than sixty adults in the college city (50,000) of Lafayette, Indiana. By faith and dogged determination, they have established the Mediation Services of Tippecanoe County, which trains and provides mediators for a reconciliation program involving court offenders and their victims and for settling other community disputes.

Leet Memorial United Methodist Church and Boyd's Grove United Methodist Church (450 members combined) are located in and near the small agricultural town of Bradford, Illinois. With two other churches in town they sponsor the Bradford Church and Community Project, which trains youth in job skills through a program of supervised home maintenance and repair services for senior citizens in the community.

Manchester Church of the Brethren is the flagship church (750 members) for the large German pietist group in Manchester, Indiana. With several church and agency partners they created Education for Conflict Resolution, which trains elementary children as mediators in conflicts among their peers. They also train adults in skills to mediate community disputes and are working to establish a community mediation center.

Martin Temple African Methodist Episcopal Zion Church is a thriving congregation of about 400 members in a middle-class African-American community in Chicago. Through the STEEP Project, the church hopes to prevent school dropouts by providing academic and cultural enrichment for elementary school children.

Millard Congregational Church, United Church of Christ/Iglesia Evangelica Unida de Cristo is a small congregation on Chicago's West Side, in which an older generation of European immigrants and newer Hispanic arrivals share. Concerned about the needs of Hispanic young people for higher education, they developed a Pre-College Program to prepare neighborhood teens for entrance examinations and college-level work.

North United Methodist Church (1,200 members), with a reputation for strong social witness, is set in a classic gothic structure located at the junction of two major arteries in Indianapolis, Indiana. The congregation's concern for young teens and their families led them to develop a program with educational, economic, social, and mentoring components.

Ridge Lutheran Church has about 350 members drawn from a pleasant, interracial, residential area of Chicago. The congregation sponsors HANDS, through which representatives from the deaf, hearing-impaired, and hearing communities advocate for the needs of the deaf and hearing-impaired.

Riverside Park United Methodist Church (seventy-five members) is located in an economically diverse African-American neighborhood in Indianapolis, Indiana. Their Riverside Park Church and Community Project offers nourishment, tutoring, and social activities to elementary age children after school.

St. Boniface Catholic Church is an old German congregation (800) operated by the Franciscans in downtown Lafayette, Indiana. In partnership with **St. Thomas Aquinas Catholic Church** and **Shalom United Church of Christ**, they provide transitional housing for low-income families through the Lafayette Transitional Housing Center and social services and advocacy for community housing needs.

St. Joan of Arc Catholic Church, which has about 1,000 families in a racially mixed area of Indianapolis, Indiana, sponsors the Neighborhood Youth Outreach, offering educational and recreational opportunities for youth along with mentoring for personal development.

St. Luke's United Methodist Church, an active congregation (750 members) with many management and supervisory personnel from the automotive industry of Kokomo, Indiana, sponsors the Literacy Coalition of Kokomo-Howard County, offering tutoring to nonreading adults, with a goal of improved employability.

St. Mary's Catholic Church, Alexandria, is a modest parish (500 families) in Alexandria, Indiana, a once thriving industrial town that has fallen on hard times. Along with a school and a community pantry, the congregation supports the Church and Community Involved Network which offers parenting education and daycare or home care for at-risk children in families under stress.

St. Mary's Catholic Church, Canton, is a blue-collar congregation in the small city of Canton, Illinois. Along with the neighboring **First Congregational United Church of Christ,** it has developed the Christian Service Program to provide assistance with health insurance claims for elderly residents. The program also offers Medicare seminars, income tax assistance, and newcomers' packets in the community.

St. Mary's Catholic Church, Indianapolis, (with a constituency much larger than its 150 families) has used its central location in Indianapolis, Indiana, to develop the Hispanic Wholistic Education Center. Their goal is to reduce the dropout rate among Hispanic students at a local vocational high school and to encourage more Hispanic youth to enroll in higher education.

South Chicago Evangelical Covenant Church, with a handful of faithful families drawn from a Chicago neighborhood of old steel mills and immigrant families, sponsors transitional housing for abused women and their children in a program called WellSpring House.

Sweet Holy Spirit Baptist Church has converted a large grocery store into a sanctuary and community building in a lower-middle income African-American community on the South Side of Chicago. One of the ministries of this large (about 2,000) and growing congregation is the CARE Center, which offers tutoring and enrichment for grammar school children from two neighborhood schools, as well as food and clothing distribution, counseling, GED classes, and programs for the elderly.

University Park Christian Church, together with three neighboring congregations, draws from a middle- to upper-income residential and college neighborhood of Indianapolis, Indiana. This coalition formed The Caring Community, which offers adult day health care and in-home respite care for dependent elderly in association with Catholic Charities, and an annual symposium on elderly health care issues.

Washburn Christian Church, although only 150 members, may be the most active church in the rural town of Washburn, Illinois. In the face of a discouraged community, with other congregations it has created Community Action Ministries. After rehabilitating a house for a low-income family, the group has tried to instill a new sense of community pride through a variety of efforts, from printing a brochure to the possible construction of a common facility.

Washington Street Presbyterian Church, a congregation of nearly 100 members in Indianapolis, Indiana, has developed Partners for Westside Housing Renewal (PWHR), assisting low-income homeowners to rehabilitate their substandard homes and joining their voices with others in a network for city-wide advocacy on housing concerns.

West Park Christian Church (fifty members) struggles to sustain a ministry in a low-income area of Anglo families in Indianapolis, Indiana. In its Teen "S" Team program the church nurtures personal and social growth by providing comfortable drop-in space for pre-teens through high school aged youth.

West Street Christian Church, the largest Protestant church (about 900 members) in the agricultural support community of Tipton, Indiana, has joined with six other Protestant and Catholic churches to develop the Mustard Seed, which provides direct assistance to low-income families along with counseling, referrals, and advocacy.

Westminster Presbyterian Church is a substantial congregation (600 members) with a tradition of social concern known throughout Peoria, Illinois. Because of its current concern about teen pregnancy, the church sponsors the Children and Parents Support (CAPS) program for single teen-aged mothers, enabling young mothers to remain in high school by providing transportation to daycare for their children and helping them to network with other social agencies.

Summary Questions
for Social Context

I. General Information about Your Community

A. Describing your community as you know it

What are the boundaries of your church/project service area?

What are the major institutions in that community?

What one social-economic feature in this community (if any) has the greatest impact on a majority of the residents? Does this have an impact on your congregation, too? If so, how?

How would you describe the community to a stranger?

B. Discovering changes and trends

Using the census data and any supplementary data you have found about your community, what were the major changes or trends in this community in the past ten years in these areas:

- population growth/decline,
- population composition: age, race, education, employment, income,
- household structure, and
- industry/economic growth/decline?

Using the current data and future projections, are those trends continuing? If not, how are the patterns changing?

C. Applying data and observations

What are some visible signs in the community of the trends that you have discerned? (This could include buildings, traffic patterns, people on the streets, etc.)

Describe the newcomers in the community. Are these persons in need and/or persons with advantages and resources? In what ways are newcomers similar to or different from long-standing residents?

Have you discovered any "invisible" persons in your community? If so, who are they? Where do they live? What do they do? Why do they remain "invisible"?

What resources, allies, and potential partners have you found, and how will your follow-up with these contacts?

D. Comparing your community with a larger area

How do the trends that you observed in your community data compare with the data for the larger area? How does the economy compare? Are the population changes similar or different? What does that suggest for your ministry?

II. Interviews with Representatives of the Community

Report at least five interviews with a representative sample of community people, including contacts among newcomers and long-standing residents, persons in business and political life, someone in planning, and persons familiar with the need groups(s) that you hope to serve. In your proposed area of service, interview at least one professional leader and at least one person (perhaps several) who might receive your services and participate in your program. To "put flesh" on the census figures, be imaginative in your interviews. For example, you might be able to interview marginalized and "invisible" people you may have found in your research. Your data may be extensive, but you need only report the summaries of these contacts in your summary report. For each interview used, give the name of the person contacted, their role in the community, and a brief summary of the key comments or insights that your group attained. Note any follow-up expected from your group.

III. Choosing a Preliminary Focus for Ministry

Given what you have learned about your community:

What is the need area that you hope to address?

What kind of ministry do you propose to develop?

How does your proposed ministry address the need?

What implications do you see for education and advocacy? For empowerment and increased self-sufficiency of the people with whom you seek to serve? For larger issues you might raise?

Summary Questions for Congregational Identity

I. Your History and Heritage

A. Your congregation's history

1. What is there in the origin (including the name) of your church that relates to your current concern for ministry in your community?

2. Give several examples (stories) of social caring in the history of your church.

3. Tell about two or three individual persons in your church's history who were (or are) "heroes" or "saints" in ministering to others.

B. Your larger faith heritage

1. What stories are there in your denomination's history that show a heritage of ministering to social needs?

2. What persons in your denominational or broader Christian heritage demonstrate the attitude of social caring that you share?

3. What statements has your denomination made regarding social needs and responsive ministries?

II. Your Theological Foundations

A. Your biblical and theological bases

Summarize the biblical and theological foundations for your concern for and approach to ministering to people's social needs.

B. Your mission statement

Summarize or quote from your church mission statement (if you have one) as it relates to your proposed ministry involvement.

III. Your Current Profile: Learnings from your membership survey

A. Correlation of congregational identity and social context

1. What have you learned from studying identity and context together that has helped you to set directions for your ministry project?

2. Given your learnings about your context and identity, and given your survey of possible social ministries, what now seems appropriate as a challenge for your congregation?

B. Congregational process

1. What have you learned about subgroups in your church and how they respond (or have responded) to this proposed ministry?

2. Given what you've learned, how will you interpret your proposed ministry, and on what basis will you receive approval and support from your congregation?

C. Development of partnerships

1. What have you learned from your identity and context about potential partnering groups, especially about your similarities and differences?

2. Given your learnings and the project area(s) in which you are interested, (a) who are your actual partners at this time and (b) who are the potential partners whom you intend to contact?

IV. Interpretating and Celebrating Your Identity

Using what you have learned from your history, heritage, theology, and membership survey, plan a worship service or other event that celebrates and embodies your congregation's identity as it relates to social ministry.

Summary Questions
for Organizing Social Ministry

I. Organizational Structure

Identify the projected organizational structure of your ministry project at its launching. Describe how you expect your organizational structure to work as your ministry project "settles in for the long haul." What elements of those outlined above will remain the same? What will change, and how?

Issues to be included:

- What will you do in your project, and how will you do it?
- When will you do it? What is your schedule for implementation? Your projected schedule for offering services? (E.g., will you operate daily? weekly? round the clock? etc.)
- Who are the partner churches or agencies working with you? How might these change as the ministry becomes established?
- Who will direct and manage the project? What will be your governing group (Core Committee, Board of Managers, etc.)?
- What will be that group's relationship to the contract and partnering churches and agencies? to the current Core Committee? to the managing staff (if any)?
- Who will make policy decisions, and how?
- What participation will there be in your managing and decision-making structures by persons from among those who are to be served?
- What legal issues or requirements, if any, need to be addressed as

you develop the organizational structure for your ministry? How will you learn about those and satisfy them?

— What are your plans for keeping records on the administration of your ministry project?

II. Personnel

Identify the staff you will need, both paid and volunteer, to get your project off the ground. Describe the staff you expect to need to keep your project running over time. What needs and positions will remain constant? What positions will phase out, and what new ones will arise?

Issues to be included:

— What paid staff positions do you expect to use? Describe these roles.
— How will you recruit persons to fill those positions?
— Who will supervise the staff persons?
— What volunteer positions will you have? Describe these roles.
— Who will supervise those volunteers?
— How will you recruit volunteers? In particular, how will you recruit volunteers from the contract and partnering congregations?
— What plans do you have for developing involvement in volunteer or paid staff roles by some of those served?
— What legal issues or requirements, if any, are there that relate to your use of paid or volunteer staff? How will you address those?
— What records will you need to keep related to your paid and volunteer staff? Who will keep those records, and how?

III. Facilities

Identify the facilities, equipment, etc., that you will need when your ministry project opens. Tell how you expect to meet those needs. Describe the facilities you expect to need over the long haul. Will your starting facilities remain adequate? How do you foresee your needs changing, and how do you expect to meet those changing needs?

Issues to be included:

— What space will your ministry project need? Where do you expect to establish it? Will you own the space? Rent it? Share it?
— What will you need to do to adapt that space to your needs? Renovate? Expand? How will you do that? Who? When?
— What furnishings and equipment will you need? Will they be donated or purchased?
— What supplies or materials will you need for operating your project?
— What participation will the contract and partnering churches have in providing for the facilities needs of your ministry project?
— How will any of those who are served become involved in filling the facilities needs of the project?
— What legal issues or requirements will you encounter in providing for the facilities needs of your project (zoning laws, building codes, etc.)? How will you meet those?
— What records related to your facilities will you need to keep? Who will keep those and how?

IV. Finances

A. Start-up: Outline your expected financial needs for the start-up phase of your ministry project. Tell how the money will be managed. Include a tentative budget.

B. Ongoing Ministry: Outline your projected financial situation for the long term of your project. How do you expect your needs to change? What continuity and what changes do you foresee in your system of financial management?

C. Fund-Raising: Describe your plans for developing a fund-raising program. Who will be involved? What types of sources might you explore? How do you expect your fund-raising program to change or remain the same over time?

Issues to be included:

— How much money do you expect to need during the start-up phase

of your ministry project (the first year)? How much do you expect
to need to continue operating in subsequent years?
— What kinds of potential resources for long-term funding have you
discovered so far in your community? (You need not name specific sources at this point, unless you have some contacts already
established. At this stage you should be exploring *types* of
sources—businesses, foundations, government grants, etc.)
— What resources do you expect the contract and partnering congregations to be able to offer to the ongoing support of the project?
— Who will be responsible for fund raising for your project? What
committee or group will do it? Will that include members of Core
Committee? Other members of the congregation(s)? Other persons from the community? What individuals have agreed to
participate in that group?
— Who will be responsible for managing the financial affairs for your
ministry project? What individuals (by name or by position) will
handle the funds? To what group(s) will they be accountable for
their management?
— What involvement do you expect representatives of those who are
served to have in the development and management of resources
for your project?
— What legal issues will you need to address related to the financing
of your project? How will you go about dealing with them?
— What plans do you have for keeping financial records for your
project? Who will be responsible for this record-keeping?

BIBLIOGRAPHY

Bloom, Dorothy. *Church Doors Open Outward: A Practical Guide to Beginning Community Ministry.* Valley Forge, PA: Judson Press, 1987.
(Basic book to orient churches toward social ministry.)

Bobo, Kim et al. *Organizing for Social Change: A Manual for Activists in the 1990s.* Washington: Seven Locks Press, 1991.
(Very practical procedures for organizing around issues.)

Brueggemann, Walter. *The Prophetic Imagination.* Philadelphia: Fortress Press, 1978.
(Strong, readable analysis of essential changes in perception as a basis for social ministy.)

Burson, Malcolm C. et al. *Discerning the Call to Social Ministry.* Washington, DC: The Alban Institute, Inc., 1990.
(Detailed account of launching a specific social ministry.)

Carroll, Jackson W. et al. *Handbook for Congregational Studies,* Nashville: Abingdon Press, 1986.
(Defines and expands the basic framework for *Basic Steps.*)

Dudley, Carl S. "Saints, Crises, and other Memories that Energize the Church." *Action Information.* Washington, DC: The Alban Institute, Inc., Jan.-Feb., Mar.-Apr., 1989.
(Describes uses of history and development of themes.)

—— and Sally A. Johnson. "Congregational Self Images for Social
Ministry." *Carriers of Faith.* Edited by Dudley, Carroll, and Wind.
Louisville: Westminster/John Knox Press, 1991.
(Expands on themes found in congregational histories.)

Fagan, Harry. *Empowerment: Skills for Parish Social Action.* New
York: Paulist Press, 1979.
(Definitions and clear procedures from a Catholic experience.)

Flanagan, Joan. *The Grass Roots Fundraising Book.* Chicago:
Contemporary Books, Inc., 1982.
(Extensive idea book from beginners to big bucks.)

Grierson, Denham. *Transforming a People of God.* Melbourne: Joint
Board of Christian Education, 1984.
(Primer in understanding congregational identity.)

Hessel, Dieter. *Social Ministry.* Philadelphia: Westminster Press, 1982.
(Various levels of involvement clearly described.)

Holland, Joe and Peter Henriot, S.J. *Social Analysis: Linking Faith and
Justice.* Mary Knoll, NY: Orbis Books, 1983.
(Hard hitting use of community analysis for social change.)

Miller, Kenneth R. and Mary Elizabeth Wilson. *The Church That Cares:
Identifying and Responding to Needs in Your Community.* Valley
Forge, PA: Judson Press, 1985.
(Step-by-step guide for a small local church committee.)

Mott, Steven Charles. *Biblical Ethics and Social Change.* New York:
Oxford Press, 1982.
(Overview of significant contemporary biblical issues.)

Pierce, Gregory F. *Activism that Makes Sense.* New York: Paulist
Press, 1984.
(Christian organizing from a Saul Alinsky perspective.)

Simpson, Dick and George Beam. *Strategies for Change.* Chicago:
Swallow, 1976.
(Three alternative ways to understand and mobilize change.)

Walrath, Douglas A. *Planning for Your Church.* Philadelphia:
   Westminster Press, 1984.
   (Practical helps for churches to reach their communities.)

Warren, Roland L. *Studying Your Community.* New York: Russell Sage
   Foundation, 1955.
   (Simple, exhaustive checklist for community study.)

Wilson, Marlene. *How to Mobilize Church Volunteers.* Minneapolis:
   Augsburg, 1983.
   (Christian wisdom for working with volunteers.)